C000183704

THE HIDDEN INNS OF THE
SOUTH EAST OF ENGLAND

INCLUDING KENT, SUSSEX AND SURREY

By Peter Long

© Travel Publishing Ltd.

Regional Hidden Places

Cambs & Lincolnshire
Chilterns
Cornwall
Derbyshire
Devon
Dorset, Hants & Isle of Wight
East Anglia
Gloucs, Wiltshire & Somerset
Heart of England
Hereford, Worcs & Shropshire
Highlands & Islands
Kent
Lake District & Cumbria
Lancashire & Cheshire
Lincolnshire & Nottinghamshire
Northumberland & Durham
Sussex
Thames Valley
Yorkshire

National Hidden Places

England
Ireland
Scotland
Wales

Hidden Inns

East Anglia
Heart of England
Lancashire & Cheshire
North of England
South
South East
South and Central Scotland
Wales
Welsh Borders
West Country
Yorkshire
Wales

Country Living Rural Guides

East Anglia
Heart of England
Ireland
North East of England
North West of England
Scotland
South
South East
Wales
West Country

Published by: Travel Publishing Ltd, 7a Apollo House, Calleva Park, Aldermaston, Berks, RG7 8TN

ISBN 1-902-00795-6

© Travel Publishing Ltd

First published 2000, second edition 2003,

Printing by: Ashford Colour Press, Gosport

Maps by: © Maps in Minutes ™ (2003)
© Crown Copyright, Ordnance Survey 2003

Editor: Peter Long

Cover Design: Lines & Words, Aldermaston

Cover Photograph: The Albion Tavern, Faversham, Kent

Text Photographs: © www.britainonview.com

All information is included by the publishers in good faith and is believed to be correct at the time of going to press. No responsibility can be accepted for errors.

FOREWORD

The *Hidden Inns* series originates from the enthusiastic suggestions of readers of the popular *Hidden Places* guides. They want to be directed to traditional inns "off the beaten track" with atmosphere and character which are so much a part of our British heritage. But they also want information on the many places of interest and activities to be found in the vicinity of the inn.

The inns or pubs reviewed in the *Hidden Inns* may have been coaching inns but have invariably been a part of the history of the village or town in which they are located. All the inns included in this guide serve food and drink and some offer the visitor overnight accommodation. A full page is devoted to each inn which contains a coloured photograph, full name, address and telephone number, directions on how to get there, a full description of the inn and its facilities and a wide range of useful information such as opening hours, food served, accommodation provided, credit cards taken and details of entertainment. *Hidden Inns* guides however are not simply pub guides. They provide the reader with helpful information on the many places of interest to visit and activities to pursue in the area in which the inn is based. This ensures that your visit to the area will not only allow you to enjoy the atmosphere of the inn but also to take in the beautiful countryside which surrounds it.

The *Hidden Inns* guides have been expertly designed for ease of use and this guide is the first to be printed in full colour. *The Hidden Inns of the South East* is divided into three chapters covering Kent, Sussex and Surrey, each of which is laid out in the same way. To identify your preferred geographical region refer to the contents page overleaf. To find a pub or inn and details of facilities they offer simply use the index to the rear of the guide or locator map at the beginning of each chapter which refers you, via a page number reference, to a full page dedicated to the specific establishment. To find a place of interest, again use the index to the rear of the book or list found at the beginning of each chapter which will guide you to a descriptive summary of the area that includes details of each place of interest.

We do hope that you will get plenty of enjoyment from visiting the inns, pubs and places of interest contained in this guide. We are always interested in what our readers think of the inns or places covered (or not covered) in our guides so please do not hesitate to write to us. This is a vital way of helping us ensure that we maintain a high standard of entry and that we are providing the right sort of information for our readers. Finally if you are planning to visit any other corner of the British Isles we would like to refer you to the list of Travel Publishing guides to be found at the rear of the book.

Travel Publishing

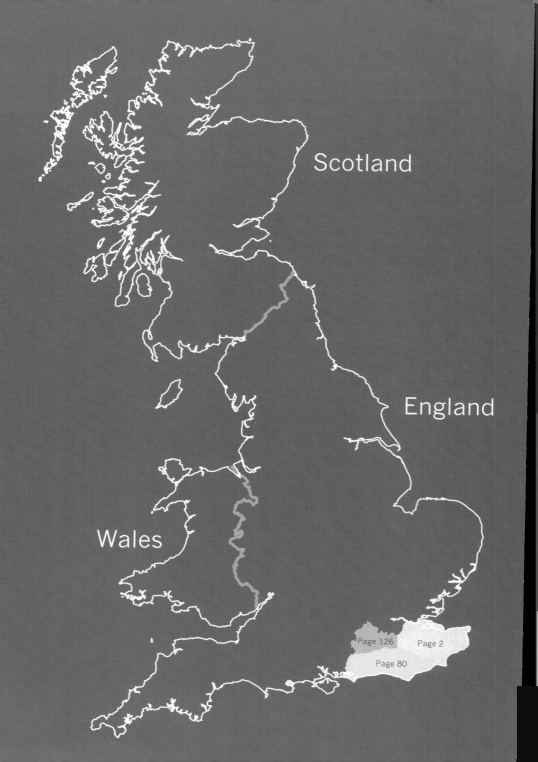

Scotland

England

Wales

CONTENTS

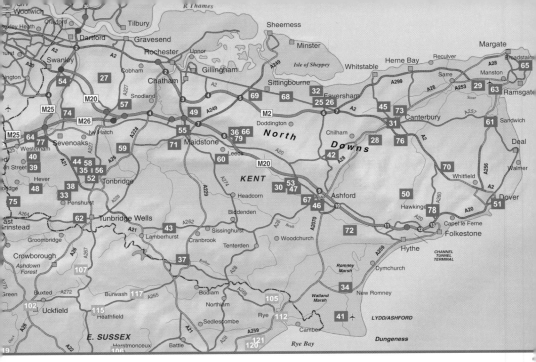

Please note all cross references refer to page numbers

KENT

Water dominates the history of Kent. A land of gardens and orchards, of historic castles and churches, of pretty villages and fine market towns, but above all it is a land, inescapably linked to the sea. Its proximity to Europe across the narrow channel means that invaders through the centuries have chosen the Kent coast as a gateway to Britain. The Romans landed here over 2,000 years ago, the Vikings followed almost a 1,000 years later and the land was widely settled by the Normans following the defeat of

PLACES OF INTEREST

Harold in 1066. All these peoples and the prehistoric tribes that preceded them have left their mark on the landscape and the language. Many place names, such as Rochester and Whitstable, are derived from Roman, Saxon or Norman origins. Norman churches and castles in various states of

Dover Castle

ruin or preservation still stand in the tranquil rural countryside that belies the bloodshed of centuries of successive invasions. The cathedral at Rochester was built on a Saxon site by William the Conqueror's architect Bishop Gundulph, and it was also he who designed the massive fortress of Rochester Castle. While this ancient city, with numerous connections with Charles Dickens, is one of the best known places along the Medway, it is Chatham that really captures the imagination. Henry VIII, looking to increase his sea power, established a dockyard at this Saxon settlement. This was the beginning of the Royal Navy that was to be instrumental in the building and

Oast Houses

maintenance of the British Empire. The Naval Dockyards at Chatham, where Nelson's ship HMS Victory was built, and the Napoleonic fortress, Fort Amherst, are two of the best monuments to the great seafaring traditions of the whole country. Further east lie the seaside towns and resorts of Whitstable, Herne Bay and Margate. Certainly the most popular is Margate, the natural destination for many people of southeast London looking for a day beside the sea. Whilst offering all the delights of the seaside, such as amusements, a fun fair, candyfloss and fish and chips, Margate is older than it seems. It is not surprising that the bathing machine was invented in the town. Whitstable, which remains famous for its oysters, presents a calmer and less brash appearance to those looking for a seaside break. With a history that goes back to Roman times, this fishing village, that became the haunt of smugglers, has managed to retain an individuality that inspired writers such as Somerset Maugham and Charles Dickens.

On the south coast the Cinque Ports were set up in the 11th century as a commercial alliance of significant ports, although silting up of channels over the centuries has left many of them several miles from the sea. Henry VIII established a dockyard at Chatham, which was the beginning of the Royal Navy and was a major factor in Britain's dominance of the seas in the centuries that followed. The whole length of the Kent coast has been the historic haven of smugglers, and every rocky cove and sheltered bay has seen daring and ruthless smugglers pursued by brave and determined but generally ineffective excise men. In villages across Kent, ancient smugglers' tales are told and houses, churches and caves are pointed out, where the smugglers' booty was hidden away. However Kent's maritime tradition did not

Kent Orchards

depend entirely on lawlessness and many villages plied a legitimate trade in fishing. Ancient fishing villages like Deal retain the quaint alleyways and traditional fishermen's cottages around the harbour areas. Whitstable has been famed for centuries for oyster fishing and Whitstable oysters are still regarded as gourmet fare. Churchill, Darwin and Charles Dickens have all had homes in Kent. Chartwell, the home of Sir Winston and Lady Churchill from the 1920s until the great statesman's death in the 1960s, has been left just as it was when the couple were still alive and it remains a lasting tribute to this extraordinary man. At Downe, just south of Farnborough, lies Down House, the home of Charles Darwin and the place where he formulated his theories of evolution and wrote his most famous work The Origin of Species by Means of Natural Selection. Geoffrey Chaucer and the Elizabethan playwright and spy Christopher Marlowe as well as Somerset Maugham and Mary Tourtel, the creator of Rupert Bear lived at Canterbury. Canterbury is the home of the Mother Church of the Anglican Communion, Canterbury Cathedral. The cathedral was founded by St Augustine in the late 6th century, along with an abbey, and both can still be seen today although the cathedral, that still dominates the city's skyline, is actually a Norman structure. The abbey and cathedral, along with St Martin's Church, the oldest parish church in England that is still in constant use, form a fascinating World Heritage Site.

The eastern stretch of the Kentish coastline supported numerous fishing villages, some of which were fortified under the threat of invasion. Deal Castle remains one of the best surviving examples of Tudor military architecture, while its contemporary, Walmer Castle, has been turned into an elegant stately house that is the home of the Lord Warden of the Cinque Ports. Dover, 'the gateway to Britain', is dominated by its massive 12th century Castle, which justifies its ranking among the greatest fortresses in Western Europe. Although Kent lies very close to the spreading suburban sprawl of Greater London, it has managed to retain a tranquil rural feel, despite commuter developments. Rolling wooded countryside is dotted with windmills and attractive villages, surrounded by orchards, market gardens, hop fields and countless gardens.

Bexleyheath

One of Bexleyheath's most famous former residents lived at **The Red House**, designed in 1859 by Philip Webb for the newly married William and Janey Morris. The interior was decorated by Webb, Morris, Burne-Jones, Madox Brown and Rossetti; William Morris described the house as 'a joyful nook of heaven in an unheavenly world'. The house has recently been acquired by the National Trust and will be open to the public from the summer of 2003.

Biddenden

Recognised as one of the finest villages in the Weald of Kent, Biddenden has an attractive main street lined with charming half-timbered houses.

At the western end of the main street stands **All Saints' Church**, founded by the Saxons; the oldest parts remaining, such as the nave, chancel and south aisle, date from the 13th century.

Bleak House

Biggin Hill

This village is best known for its association with the RAF and, in particular, with the role that the local station played in the Battle of Britain. A Spitfire and a Hurricane flank the entrance to **Biggin Hill RAF Station**. A chapel at the station commemorates the 453 pilots from Biggin Hill who lost their lives during the conflict.

Broadstairs

This family seaside resort is best known for its associations with Charles Dickens. **Bleak House** stands high up on the cliffs at the northern end of the town, overlooking the popular beach at Viking Bay. Charles Dickens spent his summers here for 20 years. He wrote *David Copperfield* here, at a desk at the window with a splendid view over the English Channel. Other famous people associated with the town include the politician Sir Edward Heath, who was born here in

1916, and another famous sailor, Sir Alec Rose, who lived in Broadstairs for many years. Writers too seem to have found inspiration along this stretch of coast as both Frank Richards, creator of Billy Bunter, and John Buchan, author of *The Thirty Nine Steps* spy thriller, lived here. Buchan wrote the story at a house called St Cuby, on Cliff Promenade, and the staircase that gave him the idea for the title still stands opposite the house. It actually has 78 steps, but this number was halved by Buchan to provide a catchier title.

Canterbury

England's most famous cathedral city, and also one of the loveliest, Canterbury lies in one of the most attractive areas of rural Kent. It was here, in AD 597, that St Augustine founded an abbey, soon after his arrival from Rome, and it was to be the root of Christianity in England. **St Augustine's Abbey** is now in ruins but there is an excellent museum and information centre on the site. The city is of course dominated by the Mother

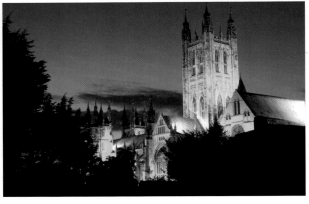

Canterbury Cathedral

discover. In the **Roman Museum** there is a fine display of remains unearthed from Dunrovernum Cantiacorum (the Roman name for Canterbury), while in the **Kent Masonic Library and Museum** the history of freemasonry over the last 300 years is explored.

There are also fine paintings, glassware and porcelain and the Cornwallis collection of documents and presentation items.

Church of the Anglican Communion, **Canterbury Cathedral**, where the tradition of welcoming visitors goes back to the days of the medieval pilgrimage. The earliest part of the present building is the crypt, which dates back to around 1100 and is the largest of its kind in the country. There is a vast amount to see here, from the splendid architecture and wonderful windows to the tombs of kings and archbishops.

It is as the scene of the murder of Archbishop Thomas à Becket that the building is best known. Becket was killed on a December evening in 1170 by the knights of Henry II, who supposedly misunderstood the king's request to be rid of this troublesome priest. A penitent Henry, full of remorse for the death of his former friend, later came here on a pilgrimage. Becket's tomb, said to have been covered in gold and jewels, was destroyed in 1538 by the agents of Henry VIII. While Canterbury is certainly dominated by its great cathedral there is much more for the visitor to

Capel le Ferne

This village, close to the cliffs between Folkestone and Dover, is home to the **Battle of Britain Memorial** that commemorates the fierce 1940 air battle that took place in the skies overhead.

Chatham

Visitors to the **Historic Dockyard** can appreciate the scale of the 20th century submarine and battleship dry docked here as well as the architecture of the most complete Georgian dockyard in the world. Rope can be seen being made in the traditional way here in the long Ropery building, and the history of the lifeboats is told at the National Collection of the RNLI.

The Chatham dockyards were an obvious target for Hitler's bombers during World War II and at **Fort Amherst Heritage Park and Caverns**, the secret underground telephone exchange that co-ordinated the air raid warnings can be seen. The country's premier Napoleonic fortress, Fort Amherst was built in 1756 to defend the naval dockyard from attack by land; its most interesting feature is the underground maze of tunnels and caverns that were used as storage, magazines, barracks and guardrooms.

Chilham

This well preserved village is one of Kent's showpiece places and is often used as a location for filming. The houses here are primarily Tudor and Jacobean and they are a delightfully haphazard mix of gabled, half-timbered houses, shops and ancient inns that date from the Middle Ages. A stopping place for pilgrims on their way to the shrine of Thomas à Becket in Canterbury Cathedral, Chilham today plays host to walkers on the nearby **North Downs Way**. The village is also the home of **Chilham Castle,** a Jacobean mansion built on to a Norman keep built on Roman foundations. The grounds around the castle were first laid out by Charles I's gardener, John Tradescant and were reworked in the 18th century by Capability Brown.

Chislehurst

Chislehurst Common is an

oasis of greenery criss-crossed by a number of small roads, but the best-known attraction hereabouts is **Chislehurst Caves**, one of Britain's most interesting networks of underground caverns. At the height of the Blitz during World War II, the caves became the world's largest air raid shelter when some 15,000 people took refuge from the German bombing raids. Visitors can take a lamplit guided tour of the various sections including the air raid shelters, the Druid Altar and the Haunted Pool.

Cobham

This picturesque village is home to one of the largest and finest houses in Kent - **Cobham Hall**, an outstanding redbrick mansion that dates from 1584. Set in 150 acres of parkland and demonstrating architectural styles from Elizabethan, Jacobean and Carolean eras and the 18th century, the house stands in beautiful gardens landscaped by Humphry Repton for the 4th Earl of Darnley. In the heart of the village stands the half-timbered **Leather Bottle Inn** that was made

Leather Bottle Inn

famous by Charles Dickens when he featured his favourite inn in the novel *The Pickwick Papers*.

Cranbrook

Cranbrook is often dubbed the 'Capital of the Kentish Weald', and one of the best places to start any exploration of the town is the **Cranbrook Museum**. In a timber-framed building dating back to 1480, the museum has displays covering many aspects of Wealden life, from agriculture and the weaving industry to Victorian and wartime memorabilia.

The parish church, **St Dunstan's**, is known locally as the 'Cathedral of the Weald' and its size reflects the former prosperity of the town. Although St Dunstan's church tower is tall, the town is dominated by the tallest smock mill in England, **Union Mill**, which is around 70 feet high.

Crayford

On the banks of the River Cray, the **World of Silk** provides visitors with an insight into the historic and traditional craft of silk making and the origins of silk are explained. Believed to have been discovered in around 1640 BC by the Empress of China, Hsi-Ling-Shi, silk found its way to Europe along the arduous silk route and, from the humble silk worm through to the beautiful printed fabrics, the whole of the story of this luxury material is explained.

Deal

This delightful fishing town has changed little in character since the 18th century thanks, in part, to its shingle rather than sandy beach, which meant that it escaped Victorian development into a full-blown seaside resort. Deal's seafront is one of the most picturesque along the southeast coast and, with its quaint alleyways, traditional fishermen's cottages and old houses, the town is well worth exploring. The **Maritime and Local History Museum** has a large collection of real and model boats, figureheads, compasses and other navigational aids, pilot's relics and memorabilia that relate to Deal's seafaring and fishing past.

On the site of the old Naval yard stands the distinctive **Timeball Tower**, built in 1795 and used to give time signals to ships in the English Channel. Not far from the Timeball Tower stands the menacing fortress of **Deal Castle**

Deal Castle

which was built by Henry VIII in the early 1540s as one of a number of forts designed to protect the south coast from invasion by the French and Spanish, angered over Henry's divorce of his Catholic wife, Catherine of Aragon. The castle was designed to resemble a Tudor rose and the distinctive 'lily-pad' shape can only really be appreciated from the air or by looking at plans of the site.

Doddington

The landscaped gardens of **Doddington Place**, in this traditional little rural village, are truly magnificent, comprising lawns, avenues and clipped yew hedges. The 10 acre garden was created by the renowned 19th century gardener William Nesfield. The display of rhododendrons and azaleas in the spring is brilliant whilst there are also large rock gardens and a formal sunken garden to view.

Dover

This ancient town, which is often referred to as the 'Gateway to England', is Britain's major cross Channel port and, as well as the freight traffic, it is from Dover that many holidaymakers set out for France and beyond. Situated high above the cliff tops, and dominating the town from almost every angle, stands **Dover Castle**, dating back to 1180. Although the castle was begun by William the Conqueror it was under Henry II that the great keep was constructed and the fortress was com-

pleted by another surrounding wall which was studded with square towers and two barbicans.

Today, the castle has much to offer the visitor. It is home to the **Princess of Wales' Royal Regiment Museum**, and there are also the remains of a Roman lighthouse and a small Saxon church within the grounds. However, one of the most spectacular sights and, one of World War II's best kept secrets, are the **Secret Wartime Tunnels** that were cut into Dover's famous white cliffs. They are now open to the public and provide the most realistic wartime experience possible. Back in the heart of Dover, in New Street, can be found another of Dover's popular attractions - the **Roman**

White Cliffs

Painted House, often dubbed Britain's buried Pompeii. An exceptionally well preserved town house, thought to date from around AD 200, the building was used as a hotel for official travellers and the excavated remains have revealed extensive wall paintings and an elaborate under-floor heating system.

Beneath the Town Hall lies the gruesome **Dover Old Town Gaol** where the horrors of Victorian prison life can be experienced. Just away from the town centre lie **The Western Heights**, a vast area that stands on what was one of the largest and strongest fortresses in the country. There are some five miles of dry ditches and numerous gun batteries and defences, and the huge complex has been preserved to include not only the defensive structures but much of the wildlife and the plants that have colonised the site down the years. One final place of interest, particularly to those who remember World War II, is the **Women's Land Army Museum,** housed on a farm, that pays tribute to the women who served their country by working on the land.

Dymchurch

At one time a quiet and secluded village, Dymchurch has become a busy seaside resort with a five mile stretch of sandy beach and all the usual amusements arcades, gift shops and cafés. However, what makes it rather different from other such resorts is the **Dymchurch Wall**, which prevents water from flooding both the town and marsh (Dymchurch lies

about seven-and-a-half feet below the level of the high tide). A barrier of some kind has existed here since Roman times.

Visitors can go from one formidable defence to another at Dymchurch as the **Martello Tower** here is, arguably, the best example of its kind in the country.

Faversham

Faversham's market place is dominated by the **Guildhall,** which was built in the 16th century. Its open ground-floor pillared arcade provided cover for the market. Unusually it has a tower at one end. After the upper floor and tower were damaged by fire in the early 19th century, it was rebuilt and extended. The town was, for 400 years, the centre of the country's explosives industry and **Chart Gunpowder Mills** is a lasting monument to the industry that thrived here between 1560 and 1934. Dating from the 18th century, and now restored, these mills are the oldest of their kind in the world. Faversham has over 400 listed buildings and rewards a lengthy visit.

Folkestone

A port and small fishing village since Saxon times, it was with the arrival of the South Eastern railway in 1842 that Folkestone began to develop into the major port and elegant resort that it is today. Within a year of the first passenger train service running, passenger ships had started to ferry people across the English Channel to Boulogne with a journey time from London to Paris of just

Folkestone Harbour

12 hours. The story of the town, from its Saxon roots right through to the present day, is told at the **Folkestone Museum** and the numerous displays and exhibits here range from the early traders, the growth of the medieval port and the town as a smugglers' haven to its development into a fashionable resort. At **Martello Tower No 3**, one of numerous such towers that were built as a defence against the possible invasion of the country by Napoleon, there is an exhibition that illustrates the measures taken to defend the south coast. The **Channel Tunnel Terminal** in England is at Folkestone, where both passenger cars and freight lorries join the trains that take them under the Channel to continental Europe.

French Street

This tiny hamlet, tucked away in the folds of narrow, wooded hills, would probably have stayed almost hidden were it not for the famous house that lies close by. In 1924, Winston Churchill purchased **Chartwell** as a family home and, with its magnificent views looking out over the Kentish Weald, it is easy to see why the great statesman said of Chartwell "I love the place - a day away from Chartwell is a day wasted." From the 1920s until his death in the 1960s, Churchill lived here with his wife and the rooms have been left exactly as they were when the couple were alive. The gardens too have been well preserved.

Gillingham

Although there is evidence of both prehistoric and Roman occupation of this area, a village did not really become established here until the 11th century, and it was the establishment of the dockyard at neighbouring Chatham in the 16th century that saw Gillingham begin to expand as it became a centre for servicing the naval dockyard and depot.

Chartwell

All things maritime have influenced Gillingham greatly over the centuries, but the town is also the home of one of the most fascinating military attractions - **The Royal Engineers Museum**. This museum reflects the diverse range of skills that the Corps has brought to bear in times of both peace and war.

Gravesend

The Thames is half a mile wide at Gravesend, where ships take on board a river pilot for the journey upstream. Much of the town was destroyed by fire in 1727, and one of the many buildings that did not survive the fire was the parish **Church of St George**, which was rebuilt in Georgian style. However the graveyard is more interesting than the church as it is thought to be the final resting place of the famous Red Indian princess, Pocahontas.

Hawkinge

Hawkinge Airfield is the home of the **Kent Battle of Britain Museum**, where the country's largest collection of 1940 related artefacts is on display. Along with the full size replicas of the planes that played such a part in the battle - a Hurricane, Spitfire and Messerschmitt have been painstakingly rebuilt from as many original parts as possible - the museum houses an important collection of both British and German flying equipment of that era.

Headcorn

This is another of the charming and ancient Wealden villages, scattered over this area of the county and, as with many of its neighbours, Headcorn was a thriving centre of cloth manufacturing. Evidence of this wealth remains in the many fine buildings to be seen here; beyond the large 14th century church, constructed of local Bethersden marble, lies **Headcorn Manor**, a magnificent Wealden house that has changed little since it was erected some 500 years ago. Just south of the village, at **Lashenden**, is the **Lashenden Air Warfare Museum** that commemorates the role played by this area of Kent during World War II and the Battle of Britain in particular. On display are numerous wartime exhibits, from both Britain and Germany, including a piloted V1 flying bomb, ration books and many photographs.

Herne Bay

Much of the town seen today was laid out in the mid 19th century as it was developed as a resort to attract Victorian middle classes looking for clean air and safe beaches. It still retains a quiet gentility, and at the **Herne Bay Museum Centre**, visitors can discover the history of the town and the story of its famous pier. The splendid **Clock Tower** on the promenade was given to Herne Bay by a wealthy London lady to commemorate Queen Victoria's coronation in 1836.

Hever

This tiny village, set in a delightfully unspoilt country-side of orchards and wood-lands, is home to one of Kent's star attractions - **Hever Castle**. The original castle was built in the 1270s by Sir Stephen de Penchester, and some two centuries later, the Bullen (or Boleyn) family purchased the property and added the

Hever Castle

comfortable Tudor manor house. Hever Castle was the childhood home of Anne Boleyn and many of her personal items are on display. In 1903, the castle was bought by the American millionaire, William Waldorf Astor, who restored the gardens and filled the house with fine collections of paintings, furniture, tapestries and objets d'art.

Hythe

Hythe is a delightful and ancient town to visit with plenty to offer visitors, particularly those inter-ested in beautiful old buildings. The skyline is dominated by the Norman tower of **St Leonard's Church**, built in 1080 but much extended in the 13th century. It has a **Crypt** where over 2,000 skulls and various other assorted human bones, dating back to before the Norman invasion, are on display.

Today, this charming place is best known as one of the terminals

for the **Romney Hythe and Dymchurch Railway**, offering passengers a 14 mile journey, by miniature steam train, across the edge of Romney Marsh to Dungeness (see under New Romney).

Ivy Hatch

Just to the south of this small village lies **Ightham Mote**, one of England's finest medieval manor houses, and long owned by the National Trust. There is plenty to

Ightham Mote

see here, from the medieval Great Hall and Tudor chapel to the Victorian housekeeper's room, the billiard room and the exhibition that details the traditional skills that were used during the major conservation programme.

Lamberhurst

Once a prosperous centre of the iron industry of the Weald, Lamberhurst is today mainly associated with viticulture, the first vineyard being established in 1972. To the east of the Lamberhurst lies **Scotney Castle**, a massive, rust-stained tower that was built by Roger de Ashburnham in 1378 and that now incorporates the ruins of a Tudor house. However, what especially draws people to Scotney are the romantic **Gardens** that are renowned for their autumn colours but are beautiful through out the seasons.

Leeds

Covering almost 1,200 years of history, **Leeds Castle** stands on two islands in the middle of the River Len and, while the peaceful moat is the home of swans and ducks, the castle itself is surrounded by beautifully landscaped gardens. Built on the site of a manor house that was owned by Saxon kings, the present castle was built just after the Norman Conquest and, when Edward I came to the throne, it became a royal palace. One of the most popular visitor attractions in

the country, it has plenty to delight and interest the public both inside and in the gardens.

Maidstone

The River Medway, on which Maidstone stands, is the ancient boundary that separated East and West Kent with the Kentish Men living in the west and the Men of Kent to the east. Maidstone has retained many handsome Elizabethan and Georgian buildings. **Chillington Manor** is a beautiful Elizabethan residence that now houses the **Maidstone Museum and Art Gallery,** founded by generous Maidstone Victorian gentlemen and holding one of the finest collections in the south east. Another part of the museum's collection can be found at **The Tyrwhitt-Drake Museum of Carriage** where visitors can see a marvellous range of horse drawn carriages that were

Archbishop's Palace

enthusiastically collected by Sir Garrard Tyrwhitt-Drake, a former mayor of the town. Opposite these stables is the **Archbishop's Palace** dating from the 14th century. Close by are the **Dungeons**, a 14th century building from which, it is alleged, Wat Tyler, leader of the Peasants' Revolt in 1381, released John Ball, the 'mad priest of Kent'.

Just north of the town centre, at **Sandling**, on the banks of the River Medway, stands **Allington Castle**, the earliest parts of which are 13th century. It was here that Henry VIII is said to have first met Anne Boleyn.

Manston

This quiet village surrounded by rich farmland that supports intensive market gardening, was, during World War II home to one of the country's major airfields. Featuring prominently in the Battle of Britain, RAF Manston was the closest airfield to the enemy coast and, as a consequence, it bore the brunt of the early Luftwaffe air attacks. The **Spitfire and Hurricane Memorial Building**, where the main attractions are the two aircraft themselves, provides visitors with an opportunity to gain an understanding of just what life was like for the pilots and other staff stationed at the airfield in the 1940s.

Margate

With its long stretch of golden sand, promenades, amusement arcades, candy floss and fun fairs, Margate is very much everyone's idea of a boisterous English seaside resort. Even before the railway brought holidaymakers in droves from London from the 1840s onwards, those looking for a day by the sea came in sailing boats known as Margate hoys. With this background as a seaside resort, it is not surprising to find that the bathing machine was invented here - in 1752, by a Quaker glover and Margate resident called Benjamin Beale.

Minster

This seaside town on the northern coast of the Isle of Sheppey seems an unlikely place to find one of the oldest sites of Christianity in England. However, it was here, on the highest point of the island, that Sexburga, the widow of a Saxon king of Kent, founded a nunnery in the late 7th century. Sacked by the Danes in 855, **Minster Abbey** was rebuilt in around 1130 when it was also re-established as a priory for Benedictine

Gatehouse · Minster Abbey

nuns. Sometime later, in the 13th century, the parish church of Minster was built, adjoining the monastic church, and so, from the Middle Ages until the Dissolution of the Monasteries, the building served as a 'double church' with the nuns worshipping in the northern half of the building and the parishioners in the other.

New Romney

Once the most important of the Cinque Ports, this attractive old town is best known as being the main stopping point on the **Romney Hythe and Dymchurch Railway**, a charming one third scale railway that was built in the 1920s for the millionaire racing driver, Captain Howey. During World War II, the railway was run by the army, who used it move both troops and supplies along the coast. Today it remains a delightful way to explore the coastline. At New Romney station can be found the **Romney Toy and Model Museum** housing a wonderful collection of toys, dolls, models, posters and photographs.

Orpington

In the heart of the town that gave its name to a famous breed of poultry stands **Bromley Museum,** an ideal starting point for exploring the area.

Close to the town centre is **Crofton Roman Villa**, built in around AD 140 and inhabited for over 250 years. Evidence of the under-floor heating arrangements, or hypocaust, can still be seen.

Penshurst

Just to the north of the village lies **Penshurst Place**, one of the best examples of 14th century architecture in the country. The house was built of local sandstone in 1341 and, in 1552, Edward

Penshurst Village

VI granted Penshurst Place to his steward and tutor, Sir William Sidney, grandfather of the Elizabethan poet, soldier and courtier, Sir Philip Sidney. The gardens are as impressive as the house. Penshurst Place also has a Toy Museum, where the world of the nursery is brought to life through an interesting collection of dolls, tin soldiers and many other toys that originally belonged to several generations of the Sidney family children.

Ramsgate

For centuries, Ramsgate was a small
fishing village until, in 1749, a harbour
was built and the town began to grow.
After George IV landed here in 1822,
(the **Obelisk** on the East Pier commemorates this historic event) the town
adopted the title of 'Royal Harbour'. By
the end of the 19th century, its fishing
fleet had grown to make it the largest
port on the south coast of England.
However, at the beginning of World War
I, the fishing industry began to decline
and, with a seemingly uncertain future,
Ramsgate enjoyed a brief moment of
national glory when, in 1940, over
40,000 British troops, evacuated from
the Dunkirk beaches by an armada of
small boats and vessels, landed here. The
town is home to the **Ramsgate Motor
Museum** where visitors are offered a trip
down memory lane and a journey back to
the days of stylish motoring. Just south of
Ramsgate lies **Pegwell Bay**, traditionally
said to have been the landing place of
Hengist and Horsa, who led the successful Jutish invasion of Kent in AD449.
The badge of Kent today has on it a
prancing white horse, the same image
under which these Jutish warriors fought.

Reculver

Reculver is the site of the Roman
Regulbium, one of the forts built in the
3rd century to defend the shores of Kent
from Saxon invasion. Sometime later the
site was taken over as a place of Christian worship and this early fort provided
the building materials for the 7th
century Saxon church that was later
extended by the Normans. It was also
around this time that the Normans built
the two huge towers, within the remains
of the Roman fort, that provided
mariners with a landmark to guide them
into the Thames estuary. Today,
Reculver Towers and Roman Fort is
under the management of English
Heritage; the towers still stand overlooking the rocky beach and can be seen for
several miles along the coast. During
World War II, the Barnes Wallace
'bouncing bomb' was tested off the coast
of Reculver.

Rochester

Rochester was first settled by the
Romans, whose Watling Street crossed
the River Medway at this point. The
saxons arrived some 500 years later, and
with the threat of a Viking invasion, it
was at Rochester that King Alfred built a
fleet of ships and thereby created the
first English navy.

Following the Norman invasion in
1066, William the Conqueror, also aware
of the importance of the town and its
port, ordered the building of a castle for
its protection. Still dominating the city
today, **Rochester Castle** is recognised as
one of the finest surviving examples of
Norman architecture in England.
William also put his architect to the task
of building **Rochester Cathedral**, on the
site of a Saxon church that was founded

Rochester Castle

Sandwich

Sandwich has its origins in
Saxon times when a town was
established here at the mouth
of the River Stour. The river
long ago silted up, and the
town now stands a couple of
miles from the coast, but its
maritime history still lives on.
It was one of the original
Cinque ports and an important
naval base, and was later a leader in the
cloth-making industry. Today, it is best
known for its championship golf course,
Royal St George's, but there's also plenty
of history, including the 16th century
Barbican Gate, and **St Bartholomew's
Hospital**, which was founded in the 12th
century and consists of a quadrangle of
almshouses grouped around an old
chapel. Just over a mile northwest of the
town is **Richborough Roman Fort**,
believed to date from AD 43. These
impressive ruins of a fort and supporting
township include the massive foundations of a triumphal arch that stood some
80 feet high.

in AD 604. Today's building still
contains the remains of the 12th century
chapter house and priory, along with
other Norman features, that, in particular, include the fine west doorway. The
Guildhall Museum covers the history of
this city from prehistoric times through
to the mid 20th century. The 17th
century Guildhall features in Dickens's
novel *Great Expectations* as the place
where Pip goes as an apprentice. The
Charles Dickens Centre, housed in an
Elizabethan building that Dickens knew
well, brings to life with the aid of the
latest technology the characters and
places of his novels.

Romney Marsh

Just the name, Romney Marsh, is enough
to conjure up images of smugglers
lugging their contraband across the misty
marshland and, for centuries, this whole
area profited from the illegal trade that
was known locally as 'owling' because of
the coded calls the smugglers used in
order to avoid the excise men.

Sarre

This sunken village on the edge of
marshland was, centuries ago, an
important harbour and ferry point when
the Isle of Thanet was indeed an island.
Today, it is home to one of the country's
few remaining commercially working
mills, **Sarre Mill**, a typical Kentish
smock windmill built in 1820 by the

Canterbury millwright John Holman.
The addition of first steam and then gas
power ensured that Sarre Mill remained
in use well into the 20th century but in
the 1940s milling ceased. Restored in the
1980s, Sarre Mill produces high quality
stoneground flour, and at certain times
visitors can explore the mill's five floors.

Sevenoaks

The first recorded mention of the town
came in 1114, when it was called
'Seovenaca' and local tradition has it
that the name refers to the clump of
seven oaks that once stood here. Long
gone, they were ceremoniously replaced
in 1955 with seven trees from Knole
Park. These replacement trees made
headline news in the autumn of 1987
when several were blown down in the
Great Storm that hit the southeast of
England in October.

The pride of Sevenoaks and, for many,
of Kent is **Knole House**, one of the
largest private homes in England, and

Knole House

surrounded by a majestic deer park.
Visitors can admire the superb carvings
and plasterwork, the Royal Stuart
furnishings and the important collection
of paintings with works by Van Dyck,
Gainsborough and Reynolds.

Sheerness

Overlooking the point where the River
Medway meets the River Thames,
Sheerness was once the site of a naval
dockyard and it was the first to be
surveyed, in the 17th century, by the
diarist Samuel Pepys, who held the
position of Secretary of the Admiralty
during the reign of Charles II. It was at
Sheerness that, in 1805, HMS Victory
docked when it brought Nelson's body
back to England after the Battle of
Trafalgar. In more recent times, Sheerness has developed into a busy container
and car ferry port and most of the Isle of
Sheppey's wealth is centred on the town.

Sissinghurst

Sissinghurst is best known
for the lovely gardens that
were the creation of the
writer Vita Sackville-West
and her husband Harold
Nicholson. When, in
1930, the couple bought
Sissinghurst Castle it was
all but a ruin. Restoring
what they could of the
castle, the couple concen-
trated on creating the

famous **Gardens** that today bring so much pleasure to visitors. Laid out in the Elizabethan style, they comprise a series of formal gardens, or 'rooms', each with a different theme such as the White Garden where only silver leafed, white flowering plants are grown.

Tenterden

The town became one of the most important centres for the manufacture of broadcloth during the Middle Ages and buildings constructed with the profits of the wool trade are still to be seen. For a real insight into the history of the town and the local area a visit to the **Tenterden and District Museum** is well worth while. The displays here cover over 1,000 years of history and they relate to hop-picking, farming, the area of the Weald, the Cinque Ports and Victorian domestic life. Tenterden is also the home of the restored **Kent and East Sussex Railway** that runs between the town and Northiam just over the county border in East Sussex.

Tonbridge

The Norman castle is certainly one of the town's oldest buildings, but its most famous institution is **Tonbridge School**, founded in 1553 by Sir Andrew Judd, Master of the Skinners' Company and a former Lord Mayor of London. The school received a charter from Elizabeth I and on Judd's death the administration was left in trust to the Skinners' Company, still the Governors.

Royal Tunbridge Wells

Surrounded by the unspoilt beauty of the Weald, Royal Tunbridge Wells is a pretty and attractive town that has been a popular place to visit for several hundred years. In 1606, the courtier, Dudley, Lord North, found the chalybeate springs with their health-giving properties, Soon, the fashionable from London were taking the waters, and in 1630, Tunbridge Wells received its first royal visitor when Queen Henrietta Maria, the wife of Charles I, came here to recuperate after giving birth to the future Charles II. Soon afterwards, enterprising local people began to build here but the real development of the town into one of the most popular spas of the 18th and 19th centuries was due to the Earl of Abergavenny. In order to increase the popularity of the spa, Beau Nash, the famous dandy who played an important role in the development of another spa town, Bath, came here as Master of Ceremonies in 1735. With Nash at the helm, guiding and even dictating fashion, Tunbridge Wells went from strength to strength; the town was granted its 'Royal' prefix in 1909 by Edward VII.

Upnor

Elizabeth I ordered the construction of several fortifications along the Medway estuary to protect her dockyard at Chatham from invasion and, in 1559, **Upnor Castle** was built. The castle saw action in 1667 when the Dutch sailed up the river with the intention of destroying the English naval fleet. The gun batteries at Upnor were the primary defence against this attack but they proved to be ineffective, as the Dutch captured the British flagship the *Royal Charles*. After this failure, the castle became a magazine and, at one time, more gunpowder was stored here than at the Tower of London. One of the guns that failed to stop the Dutch has been salvaged from the river and now stands guard outside the entrance to the fort.

Walmer

Walmer Castle was built as one of Henry VIII's line of coastal defences in the 1540s, but became over the years an elegant stately home. Today it is the official residence of the Lord Warden of the Cinque Ports, a title that has been held by William Pitt the Younger, the Duke of Wellington and Sir Winston Churchill as well as HM Queen Eliza-beth, The Queen Mother. A charming and delightful place, visitors to the castle can see the Duke of Wellington's rooms, and even his famous boots, as well as stroll around the **Gardens**.

Westerham

In the centre are two statues of British heroes who had connections with Westerham. The first is a tribute to Sir Winston Churchill, who made his home close by at Chartwell, and the other statue is that of General James Wolfe, who defeated the French at Quebec in 1759. Wolfe was born in Westerham and his childhood home, renamed **Quebec House**, stands to the east of the town centre. Nearby **Squerryes Court** is perhaps best known for its important collection of 18th century English and 17th century Dutch paintings; the sumptuously decorated rooms also house some splendid furniture, porcelain and tapestries, and one room is set aside to display mementoes relating to General Wolfe.

Whitfield

This village, which is now more a suburb of Dover, is home to the **Dover Transport Museum** where a whole range of vehicles, from bicycles to buses, can be seen along with model railways and tramways. Offering a history of the

Walmer Castle

local transport, the museum also includes exhibits on the East Kent coalfield and the area's maritime heritage.

Whitstable

Sometimes referred to as the 'Pearl of Kent', Whitstable is as famous today for its oysters as it was in Roman times and it is probable that Caesar himself enjoyed Whitstable oysters. On the harbour's East Quay, the **Oyster and Fishery Exhibition** tells the story of Whitstable's connections with seafood and fish. Visitors can also see the first commercial oyster hatchery in the world. Naturally, there are fresh Whitstable oysters and clams on the menu at the exhibition's café.

Woodchurch

One of the fine buildings to be found in this large village is **Woodchurch Windmill**, an impressive white smock mill that was constructed in 1820. Restored to full working order, the mill offers spectacular views over the marshes to the Channel coast. Also found at Woodchurch is the **South of England Rare Breeds Centre**, home to a large collection of rare British farm breeds.

THE ALBION TAVERN

29 FRONT BRENTS, FAVERSHAM, KENT ME13 7DH
TEL: 01795 591411

Directions: Faversham can be found at junction 6 of the M2.

The Albion Tavern can be found in the very oldest part of the town of Faversham, overlooking Faversham Creek. The waterside setting is delightful, with the weatherboard construction immaculately presented in brilliant white, and surrounded by weeping willows. The tow path offers an ideal opportunity to work up an appetite, while the numerous outdoor tables mean you can enjoy the peaceful setting opposite a 19th century church. Inside you will find a surprisingly spacious interior with a rural, unassuming style, furnished with pretty tables and chairs.

A very popular place, The Albion

- Mon-Sat 11.30-12.00; Sun 12.00-22.30
- High class English and French cuisine
- Visa, Access, Delta, Switch
- Beer garden, alfresco dining, car park
- Brogdale Horticultural Trust, Chilham Castle Gardens 5 miles, Canterbury 9 miles, Sittingbourne and Kemsley Light Railway 9 miles, Whitstable Bay 6 miles

Tavern attracts its clientele with fine ales and superb food. The menu is mainly of English and French cuisine, with all the dishes freshly prepared to order by a highly imaginative and talented chef. As you might expect, located not far from the coast, the chef specialises in fish and seafood dishes, with most of the key ingredients supplied by local fishermen. But be reassured, even if you don't like fish there is still plenty of choose from. Food is available lunchtime and in the evening, seven days a week. This would make an ideal treat for lunch, while you are shopping in the town, or worth seeking out in the evening. Your hostess is the charming Jenny Kent, who has had many years experience in the licensed trade, while her son Ricki is the chef.

THE ALMA

PAINTERS FORSTAL, FAVERSHAM, KENT ME13 0DU
TEL: 01795 533835

Directions: From junction 6 on the M2 take the A251 towards Faversham. Turn left at the T-junction and the next left again following signs to Painters Forstal.

On the road that passes through the heart of the charmingly-named, sleepy hamlet of Painters Forstal, you will find The Alma, a typical, weatherboard inn. Dating from the 17th century, this is a traditional style that can often be found in this corner of England. The immaculate outside leads to a cosy, welcoming interior that is largely open plan with the solid oak floors and ancient low ceilings reminding you of times past. There is a small public bar with a separate lounge and dining area, all kept spotlessly clean and bright by landlords,

Mervyn and Jill Carter. This husband and wife team have been at the helm for over thirteen years and they have worked hard to create the ambience and reputation that The Alma has come to be known for.

The bar stocks an excellent range of well kept real ales, beers, lagers, and all the usual drinks, but what makes the inn so special is the superb food that is served every lunchtime and from Tuesday to Saturday in the evening. Mervyn is the chef and the splendid menus, supplemented by the ever changing specials board, offer a mouth-watering choice of fresh, wholesome dishes that are sure to delight the whole family. The meals offer excellent value for money too. It is not surprising that The Alma is a popular inn that draws its clientele from all over Kent and beyond.

- 🕐 Mon-Sat 10.30-15.00, 18.30-23.00; Sun 12.00-15.00, 19.00-22.30
- 🍴 Fresh, home-cooked food
- £ Visa, Access, Delta, Switch, Amex, Diners
- Ⓟ Car parking, garden, children's play area
- 🎵 Monthly quiz nights, darts, bat and trap
- ❓ Brogdale Horticultural Trust 1 mile, Faversham 3 miles, Chilham Castle Gardens 5 miles, Canterbury 11 miles, Sittingbourne and Kemsley Light Railway 9 miles

ANCHOR AND HOPE

SOUTH ASH ROAD, NEW ASH GREEN, KENT TN15 7ER
TEL: 01474 872382 FAX: 01474 871188

> **Directions:** From junction 2 of the M20 take the A227 towards Gravesend. At Meopham turn left on to a minor road and continue to New Ash Green. The Anchor and Hope Inn lies in the village.

Although close to the M20 and Greater London, **The Anchor and Hope Inn** lies in a well hidden hamlet, tucked away down country lanes and surrounded by quiet countryside. Dating back to the 16th century, this attractive white weatherboarded inn, with a peg tiled roof, is a quaint reminder of the traditional building style in Kent. The large garden is popular during the summer months, when customers can enjoy the delights of the hospitality as well as the sunshine, while the interior of this ancient inn is equally inviting. With heavily beamed ceilings and walls and large open brick fireplaces, the comfortable environment of an English country pub is complete.

A friendly and welcoming place, there is an excellent selection of real ales served from the bar, while for those who are hungry, there is a delicious-sounding menu. The offering are interesting and varied with meat, seafood and vegetarian dishes that are sure to tempt the appetite. Already gaining some popularity, the new owner Geoffrey Webb has plans to expand on the food side of the business. The spacious establishment is also able to offer en-suite bed and breakfast accommodation, with six comfortably furnished rooms. Ring for details.

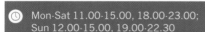

🕐 Mon-Sat 11.00-15.00, 18.00-23.00; Sun 12.00-15.00, 19.00-22.30

🍴 Bar meals and snacks

💷 Visa, Mastercard, Delta, Switch

🛏 6 en-suite rooms

🅿 Beer garden, Car parking

♪ Fortnightly quiz on Mondays

@ geoff@webbg.fsnet.co.uk

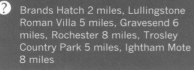
❓ Brands Hatch 2 miles, Lullingstone Roman Villa 5 miles, Gravesend 6 miles, Rochester 8 miles, Trosley Country Park 5 miles, Ightham Mote 8 miles

THE ARTICHOKE

RATTINGTON STREET, CHARTHAM, CANTERBURY, KENT CT4 7JQ
TEL: 01227 738316

Directions: From the centre of Canterbury head southwest on the A28 towards Ashford. About 3 miles out of the city you will find Chartham signposted to the left.

At the foot of the North Downs, and just off the A28 southwest of Canterbury, the village of Chartham boasts a nice mixture of old and new, being a pretty riverside village of red-tiled roofs around a church and village green. The Great Stour river led to the construction of a number of paper mills in centuries past, and for which Chartham became well known, with there still being a sizeable paper mill located here today.

Dating from the early 13th Century, the **Artichoke** once formed part of a manor house but has been in the ownership of Shepherd Neame, Kent's oldest brewery, for over 300 years. Extensive renovations were carried out during the 1990s and the full beauty of

its original medieval structure has been revealed. An ancient well was also uncovered, now forming part of the dining area, and the original beams, exposed stone walls and open fires add to the charm of this friendly village inn.

Colin and Jill Robson extend a warm welcome to all customers, old and new, with Colin manning the kitchen while Jill runs the bar. Close to the City of Canterbury, the many popular country walks make the Artichoke an ideal place to take a break and enjoy the taste of Kent with a pint of Shepherd Neame Ale.

Home-cooked, traditional English pub food is served at lunchtimes and evenings, Monday to Sunday. On fine days, food and drink can be enjoyed outside in the pleasant beer garden if you prefer.

🕐 Mon-Fri 11.00-14.30, 17.00-23.00; Sat 11.00-16.00, 19.00-23.00 Sun 12.00-17.00, 19.00-22.30

🍴 Traditional English cuisine

Ⓟ Beer garden

🎵 Occasional live music

@ colin.robson1@btinternet.co.uk

❓ Chilham village and Castle Gardens 3 miles, Canterbury 3 miles, Herne Bay 11 miles, King's Wood Forest Trail 6 miles, Druidstone Wildlife Park 5 miles

THE BELL INN

2 HIGH STREET, MINSTER-IN-THANET, KENT CT12 4BU
TEL: 01843 821274 FAX: 01843 821274

Directions: From Canterbury take the A28 towards Margate, bearing right after 8 miles onto the A253 Ramsgate road. After a mile and a half on the A253, the village of Minster will be signposted to the right.

Situated just to the west of the Abbey, on the High Street in the heart of the village of Minster, **The Bell Inn** has already enough going for it in terms of location to make it worth a stop. Visitors step inside to discover a world of low oak-beam ceilings, blazing log fires, with a murmur of conversation, in this friendly village pub. Aleks and Ian Young have run the pub for over eight years and know how to look after their customers. First time visitors will quickly become aware of the welcoming atmosphere in this characterful

establishment, which has a history dating back over 400 years, resulting in a loyal local clientele.

Food is available each lunch time with the menus offering a good choice of bar snacks and daily home-made specials, and in the evening an a la carte menu is also served with the dishes regularly updated to make the most of seasonal produce. As well as the good selection of keg lager, cider and stout stocked behind the bar, there are also four real ales kept on tap which include well-known names as well as some local varieties. There is also a fine wine list. The lovely garden is popular in the warmer months, with patrons lingering over their drinks while they enjoy the memorable views, or simply basking in the sunshine.

🕐 Mon-Sat 11.00-15.00, 18.00-23.00; Sun 12.00-15.00, 19.00-22.30

🍴 Bar meals and evening a la carte menu

£ Visa, Mastercard, Delta, Switch

🅿 Beer garden, car park

@ aleksian1@aol.com

❓ Minster Abbey, Ramsgate 4 miles, Sandwich 5 miles, Bleak House and Dickens House Museum 6 miles, Salmestone Grange 5 miles, Howletts Zoo Park 12 miles

BLACK HORSE

THE STREET, PLUCKLEY, KENT TN27 0QS
TEL: 01233 840256

Directions: From the centre of Ashford, or junction 9 of the M20, take the A20 Maidstone road for six miles. At Charing crossroads turn left towards Pluckley. Follow the road for 4 miles and the pub will be found on the left as you come down a hill.

Pluckley, according to the Guinness Book of Records at least, is the most haunted village in England, claiming more than a dozen paranormal residents. The splendid **Black Horse** pub which dominates the village has not been missed out either and is apparently home to a mischievous poltergeist that hides keys, small objects and, rather strangely, items of clothing.

The 15th century structure was at one time a farmhouse, later becoming home to the local bailiff, before eventually becoming one of the most well known of Kent's inns. The location is delightful, with the pub being surrounded by orchards and woodland gardens, in a pretty little village which gained notoriety as one of the filming locations for the TV series, the Darling Buds of May.

Venturing inside, you will discover a spacious interior that retains the original beamed ceilings and wooden floors. There is a neat bar, large lounge with open fire, a games room with pool table, and a separate, intimate restaurant. There is a resident chef who is passionate about the quality of meals served, and presents a delicious menu of freshly prepared dishes.

The house speciality is steaks, with the beef sourced locally. Food is served each lunchtime and in the evenings, Monday to Saturday. If you want to be sure of a table in the restaurant at weekends, it is advisable to ring ahead and book.

- 🕐 Mon-Sat 11.00-23.00; Sun 12.00-22.30
- 🍴 Tasty menu, specialising in locally produced steaks
- 💷 Visa, Access, Delta, Switch
- 🅿 Beer garden, children's play area, car park
- 🎵 Pub quiz Sunday nights
- ❓ Godinton Park 4 miles, Lashenden Air Warfare Museum 6 miles, Sissinghurst Castle Garden 11 miles, King's Wood Forest Trail 7 miles, Boughton Montchelsea Place 12 miles

THE BLACK HORSE

11/12 ORCHARD STREET, CANTERBURY, KENT CT2 8AP
TEL: 01227 766058

Directions: The Black Horse can be found close to the centre of Canterbury, just outside the former city walls and historic Westgate.

The Black Horse is a welcoming, friendly pub in which to stop and enjoy a drink while exploring this historic city. Beautifully presented, and totally in keeping with the rest of the street in terms of its architecture, it is perhaps surprising to learn that it was only converted into a hostelry in1909. Inside it is neat, compact and spotless with the main feature being the circular, oak bar with traditional, overhanging glass rack. The owner, and hostess, is Susan Hicks who has moved to England from Canada and made this her first venture into the

hospitality industry. With her sound business skills and bubbly personality, she has quickly made her mark and established The Black Horse as a favourite for locals and tourists of all ages.

If you like a nice pint of beer then the bar can offer a good selection of draught and bottled varieties. There is also a reasonable wine list, with everything available by the glass.

🕐 Mon-Sat 12.00-23.00; Sun 12.00-22.30

🅿 Beer garden

🎵 Live music once a month, darts, pool table

@ blackhorsekent@aol.com

❓ Canterbury, Howletts Zoo Park 2 miles, Chilham Gardens 5 miles, Herne Bay 8 miles, Bleak House and Dickens House Musuem 16 miles

CASTLE INN

OARE, NR. FAVERSHAM, KENT ME13 0PY
TEL: 01795 533674

> **Directions:** Faversham can be found at junction 6 of the M2. The village of Oare lies just a mile to the north west and is signposted from the centre.

The village of Oare lies on an arm of Faversham Creek and looks out over mainly flat marshy countryside. A one way road leads towards The Swale and at one time there was a ferry service across to Harty on the Isle of Sheppey, while the nearby windmill has been stripped of its sweeps and is now a private house, while still being a prominent local landmark. In the heart of this small village, The **Castle Inn** serves as a hub to the local community, is a popular watering hole, and has been from its beginnings in the late 19th century. The landlord, Steve Bassett, is a true beer lover and takes great pride in his cask ales. A free house, there are usually a few to choose from, with Master Brew being a regular and well-liked option. Steve has not too long been at the helm and is gradually making his mark.

Together with some fine ales, there is also tasty pub food available lunchtimes, seven days a week. The menu is mainly of traditional, English dishes, all served in hearty portions with no frills and offering good value for money. The bar areas are simply furnished, and spotlessly clean, and a conservatory dining area will be opening in early 2003.

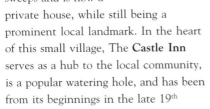

- Mon-Fri 11.00-15.00, 18.00-23.00; Sat 11.00-23.00; Sun 12.00-16.00, 19.00-22.30
- Good value pub food
- Beer garden, patio
- Occasional live music, charity nights, pub games
- South Swale Nature Reserve 1 mile, Sittinbourne and Kemsley Light Railway 7 miles, Canterbury 11 miles, Whitstable 8 miles, Leeds Castle 15 miles

THE CASTLE INN

CHIDDINGSTONE, KENT TN8 7AH
TEL: 01892 870247 FAX: 01892 870808

> **Directions:** From Tonbridge, take the B245 Hildenborough road, turning left after just over a mile onto the B2027. The village of Chiddingstone is signposted to the left after about five miles.

The village of Chiddingstone is made up of attractive 16th- and 17th-century timbered houses and, being in the care of the National Trust, remains largely unspoilt. Considered to be one of the prettiest villages in Kent, Chiddingstone has attracted numerous visitors over the years, including in recent times a number of prominent filmmakers. Room with a View, Wind in the Willows and Elizabeth "R" are among the many that have been filmed here.

In the shadow of the 'castle', you will find the appropriately named **Castle Inn**, a genuine 15th-century coaching inn of classic design. The interior is spacious with a public bar, cosy lounge and separate restaurant. Nigel Lucas, the proprietor of this charming establishment, has been here for 38 years and, together with his wife Janette, has created a well-loved drinking and eating place. Indeed, it is the food that has become king here, with the exclusive restaurant open for lunch and in the evening six days a week (restaurant closed on Tuesday) serving superb, modern European dishes. The experienced chefs use mainly locally sourced ingredients, creating a delicious menu for both the restaurant and the bar. Bar food is available throughout the day, with a Fireside menu selection in the evening. To accompany your meal there is an excellent wine list of 150 wines and a selection of real ales.

- 🕐 Mon-Sat 10.30-23.00; Sun 11.00-22.30
- 🍴 Exclusive restaurant open for lunch and dinner. Bar food. Cream Teas.
- 💷 Access, Mastercard, Visa, Delta, Amex, Diners
- 🅿 Parking on Street. Lovely garden
- 🎵 Darts
- @ e-mail: info@castleinn.co.uk website: www.castleinn.co.uk
- ❓ Chiddingstone Castle, Hever Castle 3 miles, Penshurst Place 4 miles, Chartwell 8 miles, Knole Park 9 miles, Royal Tunbridge Wells 9 miles

THE CINQUE PORTS ARMS

1 HIGH STREET, NEW ROMNEY, KENT TN28 8BU
TEL: 01797 361894 FAX: 01797 361894

> **Directions:** To reach New Romney, take junction 9 of the M20 and head into Ashford, picking up the A2070 Hastings road. After 11 miles, turn left onto the A259 which will take you right into the heart of New Romney.

It is clear from the moment you see the outside of **The Cinque Ports Arms**, with its bright red doors, colourful hanging baskets and overflowing window boxes, that this is a lively place that is well loved and looked after. It is run by Bernie and Deborah Burnett, with Bernie having decided to try his hand at running a pub after serving in the armed forces – with his bubbly personality and charm he has proved to be a natural host.

The building dates from the sixteenth

- 🕐 Summer opening: Mon-Sat 11.00-23.00; Sun 12.00-22.30, Winter Opening Mon-Sat 12.00-15.30, 18.00-23.00; Sun 12.00-15.30, 18.00-22.30
- 🍴 Served lunchtime and evening seven days a week
- 💷 Visa, Access, Delta, Switch
- 🛏 Two rooms
- 🅿 Beer garden, patio area with heaters, car park
- 🎵 Weekly pub quiz, fortnightly live music
- @ bernie.burnett@supanet.com.uk
- ❓ Romney, Hythe and Dymchurch Railway, Dungeness Power Station 6 miles, Dungeness Nature Reserve 5 miles, Port Lympne Wild Animal Park 8 milesCastle Garden 8 miles

century and can be found in the very heart of this historic, former sea-faring town providing a traditional, rustic atmosphere much loved by locals and visitors alike. The pub has been owned by the Greene King brewery since 1999 and has established a fine reputation for serving fine ales. There is a separate dining area and each lunchtime and evening you can choose from a menu of home-cooked dishes catering to all tastes, including delicious steak and kidney pie, fresh fish, and lots of locally produced fresh vegetables served with most main meals.

There are two comfortable guest rooms available, provided with tea and coffee making facilities, and hearty cooked breakfasts are served in the pub's dining room. The accommodation is clean and simple and the dedicated staff are on hand to assist in any way they can.

THE COCK HORSE

LONDON ROAD, HILDENBOROUGH, TONBRIDGE, KENT TN11 8NH
TEL: 01732 833232 FAX: 01732 834004

> **Directions:** Located directly on the B245, just a couple of miles northwest of the centre of Tonbridge.

Visitors to **The Cock Horse** can be assured of a warm friendly welcome from the owners, Glyn and Janice Jones. The couple have been here for the past seven years and established this as a popular pub attracting regular customers from the nearby towns with its good food, beer and fantastic hospitality.

A former 16th-century coaching inn, the Cock Horse presents an attractive roadside frontage of white-washed walls, topped with a traditional tiled roof, adorned with colourful hanging baskets and flowering tubs in the summer. To the rear there is an attractive garden with a barbecue, overlooking a pond and stream, which is very popular in warm weather. Inside visitors will find a traditionally styled, comfortable bar with a separate restaurant, which can seat up to 24 diners. In winter the bar is kept cosy and warm with a log-burning fire, encouraging customers to linger over their beer. Food is served at lunchtimes seven days a week, and in the evening, Tuesday to Saturday. The menu offers a wide range of meals and snacks (snacks only at Monday lunchtime), the emphasis being on locally sourced produce, with the beef and ham coming highly recommended. If you particularly wish to eat in the restaurant, it is advisable to ring ahead and book a table. The bar stocks a choice of fine quality real ales and a good selection of wines.

- Mon-Sat 11.00-15.00, 17.30-23.00; Sun 12.00-15.00, 19.00-22.30
- Cosy 24-seater restaurant
- Access, Mastercard, Visa, Delta
- Car parking, beer garden
- Great Hollanden Farm 1 mile, Knole 5 miles, Ightham Mote 4 miles, Chartwell 11 miles, Royal Tunbridge Wells 8 miles, Penshurst Place 5 miles.

THE DIRTY HABIT

UPPER STREET, HOLLINGBOURNE, NR. MAIDSTONE, KENT ME17 1UW
TEL: 01622 880880 FAX: 01622 880773

> **Directions:** Turn off the M20 at junction 8 following signs to Leeds Castle. You will shortly come to a roundabout where Hollingbourne is signposted along the B2163 to the left. Passing through the village, the Dirty Habit can be found on the right.

The Dirty Habit is a traditional English pub with a history that can be traced as far back as William the Conqueror. For many hundreds of years, this junction of Upper Street would have lain on the ancient track more generally known as the Pilgrims Way; following the murder of Thomas a Beckett in Canterbury Cathedral in 1170, pilgrims made the long journey along the route from Salisbury and Winchester. The pub's present name, adopted by the previous landlord in 1992, reflects these historic roots and is in keeping with the humour and character so well portrayed

in Chaucer's Canterbury Tales.

The Grade 2 listed building is well preserved, with many original features having been retained within, complemented by traditional, wooden furnishings. Very food orientated, the menus are excellent, with varied main courses to suit all tastes, inspired by world cuisine. Everything is of the finest quality, and freshly prepared to order, and should you have any room left there are some tantalising desserts. Your meal can be complemented by a fine glass of wine or champagne, while the bar also stocks some excellent real ales. The Dirty Habit is owned and run by Brian and Samanjitr Oke, both accomplished chefs, and they have firmly secured the pub's superb reputation as a fine eating place.

- 🕐 Mon-Sat 11.30-15.30, 18.00-23.00; Sun 12.00-16.00, 19.00-22.30
- 🍴 Fine, international cuisine
- £ Visa, Mastercard, Delta, Switch
- Ⓟ Pub garden, car park
- 🎵 Live music Monday nights
- ❓ Eyhorne Manor, Leeds Castle 1 mile, Stoneacre 3 miles, Boughton Monchelsea Place 7 miles, Kent County Showground 4 miles, Sittingbourne and Kemsley Light Railway 9 miles

EIGHT BELLS

THE MOOR, HAWKHURST, KENT TN18 4NX
TEL: 01580 753233   FAX: 01580 753383

Directions: From the centre of Maidstone, take the A229 due south towards Hastings. After 18 miles you will come to Hawkhurst and The Moor can be found just a mile further on.

Lying in the heart of the village, the **Eight Bells** is a charming 17th-century coaching inn with a long frontage, overlooking the green. Retaining much of its historic character, this attractive inn not only has a delightful country feel but to the rear there is also a secluded beer garden.

Inside, the inn is quaint and olde worlde, with open fires and the building's original ceiling beams still in place. The bar areas are well divided, providing plenty of intimate areas in

- 🕐 Mon-Sat 11.00-23.00; Sun 12.00-22.30
- 🍴 Bar meals and snacks and elegant a la carte restaurant
- 💷 Access, Mastercard, Visa, Delta
- 🛏 1 four poster, 4 twins – presently being refurbished
- 🅿 Beer garden, car park, children's play area
- 🎵 Occasional live music, jam sessions every Tuesday, satellite TV, pool, darts
- @ stm@c4.com
- ? Bedgebury National Pinetum 3 miles, Bodiam Castle 4 miles, Great Maytham Hall 7 miles, Sissinghurst Castle Garden 6 miles, Bateman's House 7 miles

which to enjoy your drink, while upstairs there is a large, elegant restaurant. Traditional bar meals and snacks are served all day, seven days a week (except Sunday night), with an a la carte menu available in the restaurant on Tuesday to Saturday evenings. There is also a superb Sunday carvery, with a choice of four meats, that is exceedingly popular. The emphasis is on fresh home-cooked dishes created from quality ingredients, and the chef is passionate about good food, which is apparent from the quality of meals served.

The surrounding area has much to offer the visitor, with numerous historic houses and gardens and some fine walking too. If you would like to linger a while to explore, then accommodation is available with a total of five guest rooms.

FLEUR·DE·LIS

HIGH STREET, LEIGH, TONBRIDGE, KENT TN11 8RL
TEL: 01732 832235

Directions: From the centre of Tonbridge, head northwest on the B245 towards Hildenborough. Turn left onto the B2027 and after two miles you will come to the village of Leigh.

In the centre of Leigh, located directly on the main road, you will find the historic **Fleur-De-Lis** public house. Dating back to the early 1800s, the classically styled building is constructed of brick with stone windows and doorways, with decorative timbered sections. Much of it is covered with Virginia creeper and in summer months the front is adorned with colourful flowering tubs.

The current licensees are Sue and Chris Anscombe, and they have done

- Mon-Thurs 11.30-15.00, 18.00-23.00; Fri-Sat 11.00-23.00; Sun 11.00-22.30
- Delicious home-cooked menu
- Access, Mastercard, Visa, Delta
- Beer garden, patio
- Monthly live jazz, regular quiz nights
- @ chris@fleur-de-lis.freeserve.co.uk
- Hall Place Gardens, Royal Tunbridge Wells 6 miles, Penshurst Place 2 miles, Knole 7 miles, Chartwell 8 miles, Hever Castle 6 miles, Long Barn 3 miles

much to update the property throughout despite not having been here long. Their love of the place shows in the care they take over every aspect of the place, and they have proved to be popular, friendly hosts. Inside, the bar areas are kept cosy with open fires, and woodblock floors add to the traditional feel. There is also a delightful restaurant, which is beautifully presented with white linen tablecloths and sparkling glassware. There is an ever-changing menu of meals and snacks catering to all tastes and appetites with a chef who has previously worked at the Savoy in London and prepares all the dishes in-house. Food is available each lunchtime and evening except Sunday evening, and at weekends bookings are advisable to avoid disappointment.

THE FOUR ELMS INN

BOUGH BEECH ROAD, FOUR ELMS, EDENBRIDGE, KENT TN8 6NE
TEL: 01732 700240

> **Directions:** From the centre of Tonbridge, take the B245 Hildenborough road, then after a mile or so turn left onto the B2027. After about 9 miles you will come to the village of Four Elms.

Dating from 1518, **The Four Elms** Inn is a traditional country pub, well situated for the M25, Chartwell, Hever Castle and local walks. The original 16th century building has been added to over the years, to create a spacious establishment with a great deal of charm.

Inside you will find three separate areas; a public bar, lounge and a dining room. Clean and bright throughout, there are open fires which add to the atmosphere.

The menu is of traditional and mostly home-cooked dishes to appeal to all tastes, all meals are well-priced and served in hearty portions and a selection of bar snacks are also available. Food is served at lunchtimes, seven days a week, and in the evenings Tuesday to Saturday. The well stocked bar offers a choice of three real ales, together with a popular selection of draught lagers and beers. At the back there is a beer garden where you can take your drinks and meals in fine weather. This is a relatively new venture for Cheryl and Victor Silvester, who run the pub with the help of their family. They have created a friendly, welcoming atmosphere where all are welcome, including children.

- 🕐 Mon-Sat 11.00-23.00; Sun 12.00-15.00 and 19.00-22.30
- 🍴 Bar meals and Dining Room
- £ Access, Mastercard, Visa, Delta
- 🅿 Car parking, beer garden
- 🎵 Darts
- ❓ Hever Castle 3 miles, Chartwell 3 miles, Starborough Castle 4 miles, Greathed Manor 6 miles, Emmetts Garden 4 miles, Detillers House 5 miles, Penshurst Place 4 miles.

FOX AND HOUNDS

TOYS HILL, NR. EDENBRIDGE, KENT TN16 1QG
TEL: 01732 750328 FAX: 01732 750328

Directions: From Sevenoaks take the A25 west for about 3 miles to Brasted. Turn left there following signs for Toys Hill. The village is just over 2 miles along the road.

The Fox and Hounds is a truly hidden place that we would heartily recommend you hunt out. It is not too far off the well-trodden tourist routes and enjoys a delightful location surrounded by National Trust land. It dates to the late 18th-century and retains a traditional feel with its

traditional white-washed front adorned with flowering baskets and tubs through the summer, while to the rear there is a pretty beer garden.

The cosy atmosphere is continued inside, with the interior being furnished with comfy sofas, armchairs, open fires

- Mon-Sat 11.00-15.00, 18.00-23.00; Sun 12.00-16.00, 19.00-22.30
- Superb food with an inventive menu
- Beer garden, car park
- Occasional folk nights, quiz nights, theme nights, pub games
- Knole 6 miles, Chartwell 1 mile, Emmetts Garden 1 mile, Quebec House 3 miles, Hever Castle 5 miles, Penshurst Place 8 miles

and a library of local books. The whole place has recently been lovingly re-vamped by the current owners, Tony and Shirley Hickmott, while retaining its old-fashioned feel. The quality of the food attracts many regular customers with deliciously inventive menus of snacks and hot meals available lunchtimes and most evenings (no food Monday night). All items on the menu are home-cooked and feature items inspired by world cuisine. The reputation is such that many diners travel from all over the surrounding area just to eat here. The restaurant is not large, so booking is advisable. To complement your meal, the bar stocks a selection of fine quality real ales.

GEORGE HOTEL

HIGH STREET, LYDD, KENT TN29 9AJ
TEL: 01797 321710

Directions: From junction 10 of the M20, head into Ashford and take the A2070 Hastings road as far as Brenzett. Turn left onto the A259 and after 3 miles turn right onto the B2075 which will take you to the centre of Lydd.

Built in 1620, during the reign of James I, on the site of an earlier tavern, **The George** has a long history and reputedly acquired some ghosts along the way. These days you can be assured of a warm welcome from owners, Tim and Ann Crompton, whether you come for a drink, a meal, a special occasion, or as a visitor to the area looking for comfortable accommodation. Under the couple's guidance, the pub has been completely revamped – inside and out. The friendly bars serve a good range of real cask ales, keg bitters, fine wines, alco-pops, and much more, and you can be sure of receiving high quality service

from the fully trained staff. After a busy day, the ideal place to relax is the Lounge Bar with a cosy log fire that is lit on cooler days, while for some lively pub entertainment you could venture into the back bar and join in a game of pool or darts.

The bar menu offers good value home-cooked food so you don't need to think twice before deciding to enjoy a lunchtime or evening meal. The newly re-opened restaurant serves a wider ranging menu of fine dishes with a non-smoking dining area. Bar meals are available all day, seven days a week, with the restaurant open each lunchtime and evening. The nine character bedrooms have also been refurbished to ensure the highest levels of comfort. The rooms are attractively furnished in a traditional style and a family room is available.

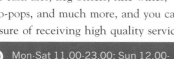

- ⏰ Mon-Sat 11.00-23.00; Sun 12.00-22.30
- 🍴 Newly opened restaurant
- 💷 Visa, Access, Delta, Switch, Amex
- 🛏 Nine rooms, including a family room
- 🅿 Beer garden, car park, pool table
- 🎵 Charity nights
- @ e-mail: tim@thegeorgelydd.com website: www.thegeorgelydd.com
- ❓ Lydd Airport 2 miles, Romney, Hythe and Dymchurch Railway 4 miles, Dungeness Power Station 4 miles, Dungeness Nature Reserve 5 miles

GEORGE INN

THE STREET, MOLASH, NR. CANTERBURY, KENT CT4 8HE
TEL: 01233 740323 FAX: 01233 740323

Directions: From the centre of Canterbury follow the A28 southwest towards Ashford. After 5 miles, at Chilham, turn right onto the A252. The village of Molash is then just over 3 miles further on.

The George is a pretty, picture postcard inn which can be found tucked away in the small village of Molash within easy reach of the M20 and M2. Here on the edge of the North Downs the village is close to woodland with some popular forest trails within easy striking distance.

The pub is family-owned and run, with Karen and John Marshall having been at the helm since 2001. The couple have worked hard to create the fine establishment you see today, with great care being taken over all aspects of the business, from the presentation of the hanging baskets to the storage of the fine ales. The beers are always excellent, with a good selection available, and the

popular favourite of Old Speckled Hen is usually available. There is a chef who is responsible for creating the fine range of fresh, homemade dishes ranging from bar snacks to a full a la carte menu which is sure to tickle any appetite. Food is served at lunchtime and in the evening Monday to Saturday and from midday until 5.30pm on Sunday. Customers can dine in the restaurant, located to one side of the main bar, though bookings are advisable at weekends. Meals can also be taken in the bar area where there is plenty of room. Dating back to the 15th century many of the original features have been retained both inside and out; the furnishings are in keeping with the character and the atmosphere is extra cosy in cool weather with a wood-burning stove.

- 🕐 Mon-Fri 11.00-15.00, 18.00-23.00; Sat 11.00-23.00; Sun 11.00-22.30
- 🍴 Wide range from snacks to a la carte
- 💷 Visa, Mastercard, Delta, Switch
- Ⓟ Beer garden, children's play area, aviary
- 🎵 Occasional live music
- ❓ Chilham Castle Gardens 3 miles, King's Wood Forest Trail 1 mile, Canterbury 8 miles, Druidstone Wildlife Park 10 miles, Godinton Park 7 miles

GREEN CROSS INN

STATION ROAD, GOUDHURST, KENT TN17 1HA
TEL: 01580 211200 FAX: 01580 212905

Directions: From Tonbridge, follow the A21 southeast for around nine miles. Turn left onto the A262 and after 3 miles you will come to the village of Goudhurst

From the road, **The Green Cross Inn** looks very much like a private, Victorian house. Many that pass by would be unaware that behind the door lies a cosy bar and a superb restaurant. The delightful establishment that you find here today is the creation of Caroline and Lou Lizzi, a charming couple that came here just two years ago. The fantastic restaurant, and the far-reaching reputation it enjoys, is the product of Italian-born Lou's talents as a classically-trained chef.

The menus are seafood based, though there are always some non-fishy dishes

- Mon-Sat 11.00-15.00, 18.00-23.00; Sun 12.00-15.00, 18.00-22.30
- Large, romantically-styled restaurant
- Access, Mastercard, Visa, Delta
- Beer garden
- Ladham House, Finchcocks 1 mile, Sissinghurst Place 5 miles, Scotney Castle 3 miles, Bettenham Manor 8 miles, Royal Tunbridge Wells 10 miles

for those that prefer. There is plenty of choice and everything is freshly prepared to order using the finest ingredients, many sourced through local producers. Food is available every lunchtime and evening, seven days a week (no food Sunday night from October to March) and once you have sampled the fayre, it is not surprising to discover that there are many regular customers. To avoid disappointment, booking is advisable.

The restaurant is intimate and romantic, with every table carefully laid out, and there is a small bar area where you can enjoy a drink before your meal. The bar is well stocked with a choice of cask ales and bitters and there is also an excellent wine list.

HALF MOON

HILDENBOROUGH, NR. TONBRIDGE, KENT TN11 9HJ
TEL: 01732 832153 FAX: 01732 832153

Directions: Hildenborough can be found just over a mile from Tonbridge, following the B245 to the northwest.

The Half Moon has been frequented as an ale house since the early 1500s and although it has always been an inn of some description, it has also seen many changes over the years. The front of the building was added in 1707, and around this time it also lay on a busy coaching route and served

as a watering hole and changing point for horses. Like many old buildings, it is rumoured to have a resident ghost who resides by the inglenook fireplace but thankfully has not been seen by the present tenants.

🕐 Mon-Sat 11.00-23.00; Sun 12.00-22.30

🍴 Delightful conservatory restaurant

💷 Access, Mastercard, Visa, Delta

🅿 Patio garden

🎵 Live music or karaoke at weekends, pool table, table football

❓ Great Hollanden Farm 1 mile, Knole Park 6 miles, Ightham Mote 4 miles, Chartwell 11 miles, Royal Tunbridge Wells 7 miles, Penshust Place 5 miles

The bright, spotless interior is open plan, retaining the original wooden floors, beamed ceilings and ornate windows. There is a delightful conservatory restaurant, and here you can sample wholesome food from the varied menu, which ranges from quick snacks to three course meals. Food is served at lunchtimes, seven days a week, and in the evening Monday to Thursday to pre-booked diners only.

For liquid refreshment, the bar offers a good selection with three real ales kept on tap, together with other popular lagers and beers, spirits and wines. The pub attracts a wide range of clientele, with a more lively atmosphere created at weekends with regular live performers or a karaoke.

HARE AND HOUNDS

4 BLEAN HILL, BLEAN, NR. CANTERBURY, KENT CT2 9EF
TEL: 01227 471594 FAX: 01227 453107

Directions: The village of Blean can be found 3 miles from the centre of Canterbury, and reached by following the A290 to the northwest.

The Hare and Hounds can be found atop a hill in the village of Brean, just a few miles from Canterbury, and located directly on the main through road. Attractively presented, this popular inn has the added feature of an Italian-style restaurant called Angelo's. This comes as no surprise when you learn that the owners are the Cascarino family, originally from Italy, coming to deepest Kent from a successful venture in County Kildare, in Ireland. Unusually, the place is open from 8.30am each morning, serving breakfast, making this an ideally positioned stopping off point for all those travelling through the area as you can be sure of

getting a refreshing beer, hot cup of coffee or something to eat at virtually any hour.

As well as serving traditional breakfasts, the restaurant offers a wide-ranging menu of hot dishes and light snacks with a distinctly Italian theme. Everything is freshly prepared, served in reasonable sized portions and sensibly priced. The main bar stocks a full range of drinks with some draught beers and bottled lagers, and there is also an excellent wine list available in both the bar and restaurant. Family-run, a warm Italian welcome is extended to all, and everything is kept neat and tidy with lots of attention to detail. The restaurant is furnished with well-spaced tables and chairs and there is seating for up to 32 diners.

- 🕐 Mon-Sat 8.30-23.00; Sun 8.30-22.30
- 🍴 Food available all day from 8.30am
- 💷 Visa, Mastercard, Delta, Switch
- 🅿 Beer garden
- @ cascarino@angelos2829.fsnet.co.uk
- ❓ Druidstone Wildlife Park, Clowes Wood Forest Walk 1 mile, Herne Bay 8 miles, Canterbury 2 miles, Chilham Castle Gardens 8 miles

HODDEN ON THE HILL

SILVERHILL ROAD, ASHFORD, KENT TN24 0NY
TEL/FAX: 01233 662226

> **Directions:** Located on the outskirts of Ashford, within 600 metres of junction 10 of the M20.

Hodden on the Hill is a quaint little establishment, tucked away on a narrow lane on the outskirts of Ashford. Well worth hunting out, the 17th century building is listed and well preserved, maintaining a real olde worlde feel. Stepping inside you enter a cosy bar with low ceilings, oak panelled walls and slab stone floors - indeed you can almost imagine you have walked into a Dickens' novel! Traditional pine tables and open fires add to the period atmosphere.

A real favourite among the locals and visitors to the town, the pub is much loved for not only the fabulous atmosphere, but also the excellent range of fine bitter, real ales and tasty home cooked food. The broad based menu and daily specials are served each lunchtime

and evening Monday to Saturday and from midday until 9pm on Sunday. Meals can be taken throughout the bar area and there is also a sizeable beer garden with 27 tables for al fresco dining when the weather permits. Hodden on the Hill is run by business partners Howard and Alison, and although they have only been here since April 2002 they run another successful pub as well. They arrange live music twice a month on a Sunday night, usually Jazz or Blues, and not too lively to disturb those preferring a quiet night out.

- 🕐 Mon-Sat 11.00-23.00; Sun 12.00-22.30
- 🍴 Fresh, home-made food
- £ Visa, Access, Delta, Switch
- Ⓟ Beer garden
- 🎵 Live Jazz and Blues twice a month
- ❓ International Station, Ashford 1 mile, Godinton Park 3 miles, Swanton Mill 1 mile, Port Lympne Wild Animal Park 7 miles, Faggs Wood Forest Walk 6 miles

THE HOP PICKERS

MAIDSTONE ROAD, HOTHFIELD, NR. ASHFORD, KENT TN26 1AR
TEL: 01233 712749 FAX: 01233 714674

Directions: From the centre of Ashford, or junction 9 of the M20, take the A20
Maidstone road and after 2 miles you will reach The Hop Pickers

---

The Hop Pickers is a large, sprawling establishment conveniently located for travellers not far from the M20. Until recently this was a hotel, but has undergone some refurbishments and improvements to create a superb, family-friendly pub and restaurant. The interior is delightfully airy and spacious with stripped wood

flooring throughout, furnished with traditional wooden furniture and decorated with dried hop bines. The whole place is kept cosy and warm in winter with open fires and an old, cast iron wood-burning stove.

🕐 Mon-Sat 11.00-23.00; Sun 12.00-22.30

🍴 Served Mon-Sat 11.00-15.00 and 18.00-22.00 Sun 12.00-16.00 and 19.00-22.00

£ Visa, Mastercard, Delta, Switch

Ⓟ Patio garden, car park

♪ Occasional live music

@ info@hoppickerspocket.co.uk

? Godinton Park 1 mile, Port Lympne Wild Animal Park 12 miles, Sissinghurst Castle Garden 13 miles, King's Wood Forest Trail 5 miles, Leeds Castle 11 miles

This is very clearly a food-orientated pub and the menus are superb. Everything sounds tempting and you can be assured that they have been prepared using the freshest available ingredients. Every taste and appetite is sure to be stimulated by the offerings. There is often fresh fish, hearty steak dishes and plenty of choice for vegetarians too. If you have room left there is also a wicked selection of desserts. To complement your meal there is a varied wine list and the bar also stocks a full range of real ales. Under the new management of Robert and Michelle Brodie there are sure to be even more improvements in the near future, though the basic principles of fine food and good ales will remain unchanged.

THE KING HENRY VIII

HEVER ROAD, HEVER, NR. EDENBRIDGE, KENT TN8 7NG
TEL: 01732 862457 FAX: 01732 867261

Directions: From Royal Tunbridge Wells follow the A264 due west towards East Grinstead. After seven miles turn right onto the B2026 signposted for Edenbridge. The village of Hever is signposted on the right after about 3 miles.

Situated within the tiny, attractive village of Hever, the **King Henry VIII** is a beautiful old English pub catering for visitors to the castle and the local community. It has recently been taken over by a delightful young couple, Paul and Buffy Warner, and they are sure to succeed here. There has been a pub under various names on this site since 1597, when one Christopher Border was indicted for keeping 'a common tippling house' without a licence, though the present structure dates back only to 1647. The traditional feel is continued inside with the spacious interior retaining a characterful atmosphere and being furnished with old wooden tables and chairs.

As well as enjoying a fine pint of real ale, you are recommended to sample the delicious food that is available all day every day. The menu offers a wide range of fresh, exciting cuisine at sensible prices and the selection usually includes some tasty steak dishes, game and home-made pies.

As well as having a long connection with the nearby castle, The Henry achieved some notoriety as being the place where the Brinksmat bullion robbery was planned. Indeed, the local police even dragged the nearby pond looking for the ill-gotten gains.

- 🕐 Mon-Sat 10.00-23.00; Sun 12.00-22.30
- 🍴 Superb licensed restaurant
- £ Access, Mastercard, Visa, Delta, Amex
- P Garden, car park, function room
- 🎵 Quiz nights, charity theme nights
- @ henrythe8th@tiscali.co.uk
- ? Hever Castle, Penshurst Place 5 miles, Chartwell 5 miles, Chiddingstone Castle 1 mile, Lingfield Park Racecourse 6 miles

KINGS ARMS

THE STREET, BOXLEY, KENT ME14 3DR
TEL: 01622 755177

> **Directions:** From the centre of Maidstone, take the A229 north, from where
> Boxley will be signposted to the right along a minor road. The King's Arms can be
> found in the centre of the village.

Despite being so close to Maidstone and two motorways, the village of Boxley lies on the edge of the North Downs, surrounded by woodland, and can justly be called 'hidden'. The **King's Arms** lies at the heart, and is an interesting building that can trace its history as far back as 1195 when it was built as a small, thatched farm building that served as a monks' hostelry. King Richard II supposedly visited in 1381 and it is his coat of arms that are depicted on the inn sign, though it did not become an ale house until 1545. Over the years, there have been numerous additions and extensions but fortunately the interior has retained its

ancient character and individual style, with oak panelled rooms, leather armchairs, coals glowing in inglenook fireplaces and low beamed ceilings.

Cosy, warm and inviting, this is just the place to come for a marvellous selection of real ales and there is also a diverse wine list. The inn's landlords, Jon and Helen Sutton, have been running The King's Arms for over 10 years and recently took over the tenancy too. They are both excellent cooks and as a result the food served here is delicious with a new and exciting menu already winning much praise. Freshly prepared in the inn's kitchens the cuisine is described as Modern English, and you can be sure of finding something to tempt even the most jaded of palates. All in all, The King's Arms is a lovely country inn that is well worth seeking out.

- 🕐 Mon-Sat 11.00-23.00; Sun 12.00-22.30
- 🍴 Bar meals, snacks and an a la carte menu
- 💷 Visa, Access, Delta, Switch
- Ⓟ Beer garden, nearby car park, outside catering
- 🎵 Regular, themed, gourmet evenings
- ❓ Boxley Abbey 1 mile, Allington Castle 2 miles, Stoneacre 4 miles, Eyhorne Manor 5 miles, Leeds Castle and Gardens 6 miles, Boughton Monchelsea Place 6 miles

KINGS ARMS

THE SQUARE, ELHAM, CANTERBURY, KENT CT4 6TJ
TEL: 01303 840242

Directions: From junction 11 of the M20 take the B2068 due north towards Canterbury. After a couple of miles the village of Elham will be signposted to the right and will be reached after about 4 miles.

Dating back to the 15th century, the **Kings Arms** is one of the oldest buildings in the village of Elham, where it stands proudly in the main square looking directly onto the very old church. Centuries ago it was known as the Cock Inn, when a part of the premises was used for cock fighting. Now a charming country pub, tucked away in the North Downs, the current owners are business partners Barry Preston and Debbi Howells and they have worked hard to get the place just as they like it.

It is plain to see that great efforts have

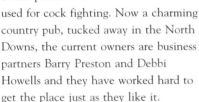

🕐 Mon-Sat 11.00-15.00, 18.00-23.00; Sun 11.00-15.00, 18.00-22.30

🍴 Traditional English cuisine

💷 Visa, Mastercard, Delta, Switch

🅿 Beer garden, disabled access

❓ West Wood Forest Walks 3 miles, Kent Battle of Britain Museum 4 miles, Romney Hythe and Dymchurch Railway 8 miles, Port Lympne Wild Animal Park 9 miles

been made to improve the interior resulting in a neat lounge bar with a separate dining area.

Here you can enjoy a fine pint of real ale with the bar stocking a few choice ales, including some excellent Harveys Best. Of course there are also some draught and bottled lagers, spirits and soft drinks together with an ever increasing wine list.

Food is served at lunchtime seven days a week and each evening except Sunday. The wide-ranging menu offers mainly traditional English cuisine, all home-made and freshly prepared to order, and the steak and kidney pie is particularly recommended.

THE LORD NELSON

FLYING HORSE LANE, DOVER, KENT CT16 1NT
TEL: 01304 204369

> **Directions:** From the end of the M20, the town of Dover can be found 7 miles along the A20.

From the 1700s, **The Lord Nelson** public house has been a well-respected landmark within the town of Dover. A truly classic English pub, it is in fact one of the oldest pubs in Dover and here you can experience the friendly atmosphere and warm welcome that makes it so popular. The landlord, Jim Turner, took on the place just two years ago having previously been a milkman, and has gradually refurbished the whole building and made it much more of a family-friendly pub, catering to a wide-ranging clientele of all ages and interests.

The Lord Nelson is part of Shepherd Neame brewery and here you can experience two of Britain's finest real ales. Try the distinctive taste of the classic bitter, Masterbrew, or the refined premium ale, Spitfire, both brewed locally in Kent. For those who prefer, the bar also has draught and bottled lager, wine, spirits and soft drinks. You can enjoy your drinks in the spacious public bar, cosy lounge or in the delightful conservatory, which adjoins a patio garden area overlooking the River Dour. There is a reasonable variety of food available between midday and 4pm daily, from a menu of traditional bar meals and snacks including children's selection and home-made sandwiches.

The Lord Nelson is only 20 minutes from the ferry terminal, behind the tourist information office, and only two minutes walk from the town centre.

- 🕐 Mon-Sat 11.00-23.00; Sun 12.00-22.30
- 🍴 Bar meals and snacks each lunchtime
- 🅿 Patio garden, disabled facilities
- 🎵 Live music Thursdays, Disco Friday and Saturday, darts, pool
- ❓ Dover Castle, Dover Museum, Kent Battle of Britain Museum 8 miles, Walmer Castle and Gardens 7 miles, Port Lympne Wild Animal Park 16 miles

MAN OF KENT

14 EAST STREET, TONBRIDGE, KENT TN9 1HG
TEL: 01732 371920   FAX: 01732 362635

Directions: East Street can be found just off the High Street in the centre of Tonbridge.

The Man of Kent is a town centre pub located just 100 metres off the High Street. Dating back to the 15th century it is a listed building and has been lovingly maintained throughout. In summer it is tastefully decked out with flowering baskets while in winter the atmosphere inside is kept cosy with a woodburning stove. The interior has a traditional feel with low ceilings, oak beams and ornate windows, and furnished with old wooden tables and chairs.

- 🕐 Mon-Sat 11.00-23.00; Sun 12.00-22.30
- 🍺 Good pub food
- 💷 Access, Mastercard, Visa, Delta
- 🅿 Beer garden, wheelchair access
- 🎵 Karaoke every other Saturday and occasional disco, juke box, darts, Sky TV
- @ stgeorgestavern@aol.com
- ❓ Tonbridge Castle, Museum, Royal Tunbridge Wells 5 miles, Penshurst Place 5 miles, Chartwell 11 miles, Emmetts Garden 10 miles, Knole Park 7 miles

The well stocked bar offers a selection of three cask ales, a good wine list and a wide choice of designer beers. A traditional menu of pub food is served from 12noon to 5pm, six days a week, and only the freshest ingredients are used to create well-presented dishes, with a menu catering to all tastes and appetites. To the rear there is a good-sized beer garden with seven tables where you can make the most of sunny days and warm weather. Your charming hostess is Gill Hooper, who has only recently taken over 'The Man'. A local lady, she has many years' experience running pubs in London. She plans a lively programme of musical events with regular karaoke nights and discos.

OLDE KINGS HEAD

THE STREET, HOTHFIELD, NR. ASHFORD, KENT TN26 1ES
TEL: 01233 640319

> **Directions:** From the centre of Ashford, or junction 9 of the M20, take the A20
> Maidstone road. The village of Hothfield will be signposted on the left.

The Olde Kings Head is a sturdy, red-brick building which dates back to the late 17th century and enjoys a prominent location within the village of Hothfield. Newly taken over by Debra Perkins, a former manager for Scottish and Newcastle brewery,

there clearly isn't much she doesn't know about beer. She is making her mark on the pub too, bringing it to life with a gradual refurbishment of the premises both inside and out, while retaining its best features.

A popular village hostelry, a friendly welcome is extended to all newcomers, and here you can be assured of comfortable surroundings in which to enjoy a quiet drink and a bite to eat. The bar stocks a good choice of draught beers and a very fine mild which is popular too. The food is good value, traditional pub fayre served with no frills; just tasty and fresh. The menu of bar meals is served each lunchtime and until 10pm in the evening, seven days a week, in the bar and the separate Kings Restaurant, with a selection of snacks available through the afternoon as well. Most of the time it is nice and quiet here, but there is a regular programme of live performers each Saturday night.

- Mon-Sat 11.30-23.00; Sun 12.00-22.30
- Good value food, with snacks available all day
- Beer garden
- Live music on Saturday nights
- Godinton Park 1 mile, International Station 4 miles, Sissinghurst Castle Garden 13 miles, King's Wood Forest Trail 5 miles, Lashenden Air Warfare Museum 9 miles

PIED BULL

Kent

HIGH STREET, FARNINGHAM, KENT DA4 0DG
TEL: 01322 862125

Directions: Farningham is located on the A20 just over a mile from the junction of the M25 and the M20.

Built in the 17th century, the **Pied Bull** was originally a coaching inn on the busy London to Maidstone route with as many as six coaches a day using it as a watering hole. This history is undoubtedly the foundation of the stories of ghostly sounds of a coach and horses being heard here on occasion. Thankfully, the coach and horses have long gone, and the ghosts aren't heard often, and the main route to Maidstone is now along the M20.

Very traditional in its styling, the pub is a prominent feature of the village's High Street and has to one side a pretty beer garden. Inside, the interior is comfortable and well furnished with chunky oak tables, stone floors, thick carpets and open fires. The current owners, Sue and Brian Lemon, have been here for over two years and ensured a steady clientele of regular customers from the surrounding area. Much of the pub's popularity is due to the superb selection of food that is available at lunchtimes, Tuesday to Sunday, and in the evenings by advance booking only. The menu can only be described as breathtaking, and it would be best to arrive in good time as it could take you a while to decide what to have. In motorcycling circles the pub is well known for the annual Boxing Day run held there.

- ⏲ Mon 15.00-23.00; Tues-Sat 11.00-23.00; Sun 12.00-22.30
- 🍴 Superb menus, bookings only in evening
- £ Visa, Mastercard, Delta, Switch
- Ⓟ Beer garden, car park
- ♫ Occasional live music
- @ brian@pied-bull.co.uk
- ❓ Lullingstone Castle 3 miles, Brands Hatch Racing Track 3 miles, Biggin Hill Airfield 12 miles, Down House 11 miles, Sevenoaks 7 miles, Ightham Mote 11 miles

THE PILOT

23-25 UPPER STONE STREET, MAIDSTONE, KENT ME15 6EU
TEL: 01622 691162 FAX: 01622 691162

Directions: Located within the centre of Maidstone, just a couple of miles from junction 5 of the M20.

The Pilot is housed within a genuine 16th century building which has been completely restored and upgraded, resulting in it becoming a prominent feature in an otherwise rather drab street within the town. A traditional, town centre pub, here you can enjoy a refreshing Harveys real ale, a cold drink or something tasty to eat. The ales are certainly worth stopping for here, with The Pilot being awarded the title 'Maidstone and Mid-Kent Pub of the Year' by the local branch of CAMRA. In recent years the pub has won the title twice and been the runner-up twice, so it is certainly doing something right.

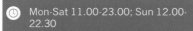

- 🕐 Mon-Sat 11.00-23.00; Sun 12.00-22.30
- 🍴 Simple, good value, pub food
- 🅿 Beer garden, barbeque
- 🎵 Live music each Sunday, piano, petanque pitch
- ❓ Allington Castle, Boughton Monchelsea Place 4 miles, Eyhorne Manor 5 miles, Leeds Castle 6 miles, Kent County Showground 6 miles, Stoneacre 3 miles

The current owners are Laurence and Heather Francis, and Laurence's former career as a musician has resulted in the introduction of live performers on a regular basis. The couple are also responsible for the fine menu of simple, pub food which is available each lunchtime and evening, except Sunday night. The menus change regularly and are supplemented by daily specials while the Sunday lunchtime music is popular so advance booking is to be recommended. Meals can be taken in the bright and pleasant dining area, while there is also a cosy lounge bar with big open fire. To while away a wet afternoon or cold evening there are a number of pub games provided including a Sunday evening quiz and petanque.

THE PINNACLES

SHIPBOURNE ROAD, TONBRIDGE, KENT TN10 3EL
TEL: 01732 770308 FAX: 01732 770076

Directions: From junction 5 on the M25 take the A21 and then the A2014 into Tonbridge. The Pinnacles can be found on the A227 on the outskirts of the town.

Located on a large corner site, on the outskirts of Tonbridge, **The Pinnacles** is an attractive, eyecatching inn that is hard to miss. Bedecked with hanging baskets during the summer and with colourful flower beds at the front, the entrance to this early 1800s building is surrounded by a splendid pergola. Starting life as a house, hotel and stables, this charming pub acquired its name as it lies, according to the Ordnance Survey Map, on the pinnacle of north Tonbridge. A large and spacious inn, the light and airy atmosphere inside is created by the open plan design, complemented by

conservatory style dining area. A lively and friendly pub, where customers can be sure of being served by attentive and helpful staff, the bar and the dining area look out onto the pretty beer garden.

The new owners are business partners Roy Walker and Clare Ward, who have been waiting quite some time to take over. Arriving in 2002 they have plans to upgrade the décor throughout and also to introduce completely new food menus. A menu of light meals and bar snacks will shortly be introduced, available every day. What makes The Pinnacles so special is the lively atmosphere here - there is always something going on. The big screen TV shows major football matches, and other sporting events, and there is live music each Friday and Saturday night.

- Mon-Sat 11.00-23.00; Sun 12.00-22.30
- Sunday lunch, and snacks at all other times
- Visa, Mastercard, Delta, Switch
- Large beer garden, car park
- Live music Friday and Saturday nights, pool, big screen TV
- Tonbridge Castle, Hall Place Gardens 3 miles, Ightham Mote 4 miles, Penshurst Place 5 miles, Knole Park 7 miles, Chartwell House 10 miles

THE PLOUGH

TAYLORS LANE, TROTTISCLIFFE, WEST MALLING, KENT ME19 5DR
TEL: 01732 822233

> **Directions:** From junction 2 of the M20, pick up the A20 Maidstone road. After 1 mile, at a roundabout, bear left onto the A227 signposted for Gravesend, turning right almost immediately following signs for Trottiscliffe.

The village of Trottiscliffe, pronounced 'Trosley', by the locals, is a quaint little place of narrow lanes and pretty cottages, well off the beaten track and nestling on the southern side of the North Downs. **The Plough** is a charming family-run pub which dates back to the 15th century when it was originally two farm cottages, not becoming an alehouse until the early 1800s. Its more recent history concerns Anne and David Dyer, a mother and son team, who took over the place in 2000, with Anne being responsible for the superb food that is served and David running the bar.

Everyone is invited to soak up the

friendly atmosphere in the cosy, olde worlde surroundings of the bar where you will find oak beams and open log fires adding to the ambience. Here, and in the newly refurbished lounge/dining area, you can sample the superb cuisine, real ales and fine wines. Bar snacks and home cooked meals are available throughout the week, at lunchtime and in the evening, with the exception of Sunday and Monday evenings. The wide ranging menu encompasses fresh fish and home-made pies and daily specials, all prepared using locally purchased produce. Booking in advance is always recommended if you want to be sure of getting a table. You can enjoy live music here on the second and last Wednesday of each month, with the theme usually being 60s and 70s music.

- 🕐 Mon-Fri 11.30-14.30, 18.00-23.00; Sat 11.30-14.30, 18.30-23.00; Sun 12.00-16.00
- 🍴 Wide ranging menu of home-made dishes
- 💷 Visa, Access, Delta, Switch
- 🅿 Beer garden, patio, car park
- 🎵 Live music twice monthly
- ❓ Ightham Mote 7 miles, Knole House 9 miles, Mere House Gardens 6 miles, Cobham village 7 miles, Owletts House 7 miles, Brands Hatch 7 miles, Lullingstone Castle and Roman Villa 11 miles

THE PLOUGH & GREAT BARN

LEIGH ROAD, HILDENBOROUGH, NR. TONBRIDGE, KENT TN11 9AJ
TEL: 01732 832149 FAX: 01732 832149

Directions: Located directly on the B245, just a couple of miles northwest of the centre of Tonbridge

The Plough is a delightful, 16th-century country pub, which enjoys a quiet location set back from the main road, yet within easy reach of the main transport links. The quaint building is of a traditional, local style with very ornate, original window-panes. The historic feel is continued inside, with the original stone-faced walls, beamed ceilings, wood-block floors and open log fires contributing to the cosy atmosphere. The furniture also has a well-used feel, with old oak tables and chairs throughout. There is a well-maintained, private garden outside which is great for al fresco drinking and eating in the summer.

- 🕐 Mon-Sat 12.00-15.00, 18.00-23.00; Sun 12.00-22.30
- 🍴 High quality food for all tastes
- £ Access, Mastercard, Visa, Delta
- Ⓟ Large beer garden, function suite, childrens playground
- @ theplough@hildenborough.fsworld.com
- ❓ Great Hollanden Farm 1 mile, Knole Park 5 miles, Ightham Mote 4 miles, Chartwell 11 miles, Royal Tunbridge Wells 8 miles, Penshust Place 5 miles

Here you can enjoy a quiet, refreshing drink with the bar offering Harveys Best as one of the three real ales, together with some other lagers, beers, spirits and soft drinks. Tasty, home-cooked food is available from a wide-ranging menu offering plenty of choice to suit all tastes and appetites. There is also a superb Sunday carvery, which is excellent value for money. To complement your meal there is a well-balanced wine list to choose from.

Attached to the pub is a barn, which is available for private parties and functions; with its own bar it can be separated from the rest of the pub. The Plough also boasts wedding reception facilities and a large garden, so this could prove to be an ideal choice for a venue for your special day.

THE QUEENS HEAD

BUTCHERS LANE, MEREWORTH, KENT ME18 5QD
TEL: 01622 812534

> **Directions:** From the M20, leave at junction 4 and head due south on the A228. After just over 4 miles is the village of Mereworth.

About a mile from the village, positioned on a gentle hill, you will find **The Queens Head**; a friendly, welcoming establishment run by Annette and Glenn Belcher. The couple have been here just two years and have worked hard to bring the whole place up to scratch by refurbishing it inside and out. The pub is conveniently located not far from the major road links yet is tucked away in a quiet corner away from the hustle and bustle. The building dates from the early 19th century and has a freshly painted exterior, decorated with hanging baskets, while inside you will find simple furnishings combined with

brightly coloured walls, creating a clean, airy ambiance.

Open all day every day, children and parties of walkers are welcome along with locals and visitors to the area who frequent The Queens Head for its fine bitters and tasty home-cooked food. The menu is of mainly traditional English cuisine; simple dishes served with no frills, in hearty portions and offering excellent value for money. Food is served midday-2pm and 6-9pm, seven days a week, and if you haven't time to stop there is also a take away service available. For a livelier night out then ring and ask about the occasional theme nights as there is usually at least one each month.

- Mon-Sat 12.00-23.00; Sun 12.00-22.30
- Good value, traditional food with take away service
- Patio garden, car park
- Occasional theme nights
- Mere House Gardens, Dene Park Forest Walk 5 miles, Maidstone 7 miles, Boughton Montchelsea Place 8 miles, Leeds Castle 13 miles, Ightham Mote 7 miles

THE QUEENS HEAD

HIGH STREET, SUTTON VALENCE, KENT ME17 3AG
TEL: 01622 843225 FAX: 01622 843225

Directions: Leaving the M20 at junction 8, take the Leeds road through Langley and out the other side. Just as you are leaving the town turn left onto the A274. Crossing over the B2163, the village of Sutton Valence is just over one mile further on.

Tucked away on a partially cobbled street in the village of Sutton Valance you will find the elegant establishment of **The Queens Head**. Dating from the 15th century the pub was almost certainly a coaching inn at one time, and it is not hard to imagine the coaches and horses pulling up outside. The whole building is immaculately maintained by the current owner Barrie Williams, who runs the place with his charming Danish wife, Lena.

Inside the atmosphere is cosy and intimate, with the plush carpet and huge log fires adding to the comfortable feel. Popular with the locals, and attracting regular customers from nearby Maidstone, the pub serves some fine ales and tasty home-cooked food. The menu caters to all tastes, with delicious steaks, home-made pies and vegetarian dishes too. To accompany your meal there is also an excellent selection of wines. Food is served every lunchtime and most evenings (no food Sunday or Monday nights).

Clean, comfortable accommodation is available with four guest rooms. They all share a large bathroom and are provided with tea and coffee making facilities.

- Mon 17.30-23.00; Tue-Sat 12.00-23.00; Sun 12.00-22.30
- Home-cooked, tasty dishes
- Visa, Access, Delta, Switch
- Four rooms
- Beer garden, car park
- Boughton Monchelsea 3 miles, Leeds Castle 4 miles, Stoneacre 3 miles, Lashenden Air Warfare Museum 5 miles, Sissinghurst 10 miles, Maidstone 6 miles

THE RED COW

12 MOAT SOLE, SANDWICH, KENT CT13 9AU
TEL: 01304 613243

Directions: From Canterbury follow the A257 due east to the town of Sandwich.

Tom and Di Savage welcome one and all to the 16th-century **Red Cow Inn**, situated within the picturesque mediaeval cinque port of Sandwich - once one of the busiest and largest ports in England. The pub is thought to have originally been a monk's retreat before becoming a poor house and then a public house in the 1800's. The name of the pub is believed to have originated from the Herefordshire breed of cows, known as 'Red Cows', often sold in the adjacent cattle market.

Located in the heart of the old town, on a narrow street full of ancient buildings, the pub's garden is a secluded haven away from the hustle and bustle and where, on fine days, you can relax and enjoy a refreshing drink, some food and the friendly atmosphere. Inside, the layout allows space in which to have a quiet drink while not feeling too cramped either. The lounge bar area is kept cosy with an open fire and attractively furnished with wooden table and chairs, with a separate 24-seater restaurant area. The extensively stocked bar has a wide range of real ales, including Greene King IPA, together with popular lagers and ciders and there is a good wine list too. Enjoy a wide variety of home cooked food either from the bar or in the restaurant every evening (except Sunday evening) but bear in mind, the kitchen closes at 2pm and 9.30pm each day. The wide-ranging menu includes traditional favourites, fresh fish, home-cooked pies, pasta and vegetarian dishes. Well-behaved children are welcome lunchtimes and early evenings in the restaurant and the garden.

- Mon-Sat 11.00-14.30, 18.00-23.00; Sun 12.00-15.00, 19.00-22.30
- Home-cooked dishes, specialising in fresh fish
- Visa, Mastercard, Delta, Switch
- Beer garden
- e-mail: savtom@dialstart.net website: www.theredcow.co.uk
- Sandwich, Canterbury 13 miles, Northbourne Court Gardens 4 miles, Pegwell Bay Nature Reserve 3 miles, Deal Castle 5 miles

THE RED LION

LOWER GREEN ROAD, RUSTHALL, ROYAL TUNBRIDGE WELLS,
KENT TN4 8TT
TEL: 01892 520086

Directions: The village of Rusthall can be found just over one mile from Royal Tunbridge Wells, heading west on the A264.

The Red Lion is very much a family-run pub, managed primarily by Martin, the landlord and chef, Ann, the landlady, and their son and daughter, Andrew and Emma. The family have only been here for a year but the pub itself has a long history going back over 600 years. The first license to sell alcoholic beverages was acquired in 1415, making it Kent's oldest licensed public house, so it seems quite appropriate that the pub is owned by Britain's oldest working brewery - Shepherd Neame.

The original 15th-century building has retained a traditional interior with low, beamed ceilings and a wood-block floor all adding to the cosy, old-fashioned atmosphere. Here visitors can enjoy a pint of real ale from the well-stocked bar, or a tasty, home-cooked meal from the kitchens. There is a small restaurant, although meals can also be taken in the bar, and food is available every lunchtime and evening (no food on Sunday evening). The spacious beer garden is popular in summer months, especially with families with children, because here you will find a bouncy castle and children's play area.

- 🕐 Mon-Sat 12.00-15.30, 17.30-23.00; Sat 11.00-23.00; Sun 11.00-22.30
- 🍴 Tasty home-cooked food
- 💷 Access, Mastercard, Visa, Delta
- Ⓟ Beer garden, children's play area, car park
- ♫ Live music on Friday nights, monthly pub quiz, themed food nights, BBQ, darts
- @ www.redlionrusthall.co.uk
- ❓ Royal Tunbridge Wells 1 mile, Penshurst Place 5 miles, Bowles Outdoor Pursuit Centre 5 miles, Bayham Abbey 5 miles, Scotney Castle 7 miles

THE SPORTSMAN

123 SANDWICH ROAD, CLIFFSEND, RAMSGATE, KENT CT12 5JB
TEL: 01843 592175 FAX: 01843 599537

> **Directions:** From Canterbury take the A28 towards Margate, bearing right onto the A253 after 8 miles, following the signs to Ramsgate. Just on the outskirts of Ramsgate, pick up the A256 Sandwich Road. Almost immediately you will find Cliffs End, and The Sportsman on your right.

The Sportsman is a friendly, family-run pub enjoying a fine position on the main seafront road between Ramsgate and Sandwich looking out over the English Channel. With origins in the 18th century it has an old-fashioned and down to earth atmosphere where

everyone, young and old, are sure to feel right at home. The regular clientele is made up of locals and visitors to the area, and they all mingle at the spacious bar.

- 🕐 Mon-Sat 11.00-23.00; Sun 12.00-22.30
- 🍴 Home-made food with no frills
- 🅿 Patio garden, function room, car park
- 🎵 Regular live music, charity events, darts, pool table
- @ abtommy@aol.com
- ❓ Sandwich 4 miles, Ramsgate 3 miles, Bleak House and Dickens House Museum 4 miles, Salmestone Grange 5 miles, Howletts Zoo Park 12 miles

This is a Shepherd Neame pub, so you can be sure of there being an excellent range of cask ales and lagers on offer. The food is all home-made and the freshness of the ingredients can be guaranteed. The regular menu includes some popular favourites, with the house speciality being Steak and Ale pie, supplemented by a daily specials board. Food is served lunchtime and in the evening each day. The owners are husband and wife team, Derek and Allison Boot, with Allison directing operations in the kitchen and Derek looking after everything else. They have created a super, family-friendly pub where everyone can feel right at home. Well behaved dogs are welcome.

THE STANHOPE ARMS

CHURCH ROAD, BRASTED, KENT TN16 1HZ
TEL: 01959 562929

> **Directions:** Brasted can be found just three miles due west of Sevenoaks on the A25

The Stanhope Arms is set slightly above the village and reached by a tiny little road, and we think it is well worth going the extra distance. The pub is built on a site that dates back to 917 when the adjoining church was constructed, though the structure you see today is somewhat newer, dating from the 1300s. The interior is gradually undergoing some refurbishments, though the place is already clean, bright, spacious and welcoming.

Described as a traditional local's local, a warm welcome is extended to customers old and new by the landlords, Robert and Beverley Playter. In fact, it is the locals that swear by the quality of the IPA Greene King ale that is kept on tap – apparently it is the finest in the area. The menu is mainly traditional pub food,

presented with no frills, just fresh, simple and offering good value for money. Food is available in the main bar, the games room and the separate dining room. Outside there is a large beer garden which is the ideal place for enjoying a drink or family meal while keeping an eye on the children. There is also a barbeque area which is available by request.

One of the oldest known pub games, which originated in Canterbury and Maidstone over 400 years ago, is Bat and Trap. Information on the game, and all the facilities for playing it, are available here. The Stanhope Arms has a local team, so why not visit and watch a game being played, or arrange to play a game with friends.

- Mon-Wed 11.00-15.00, 18.00-23.00; Thurs-Sat 11.00-23.00; Sun 11.00-22.30
- Simple, value for money, food
- Access, Mastercard, Visa, Delta
- Beer garden
- Quiz nights
- Robert@playter.freeserve.co.uk
- Knole 5 miles, Chartwell 3 miles, Emmetts Garden 2 miles, Quebec House 2 miles, Hever Castle 8 miles, Ightham Mote 9 miles

THE STAR INN

460 MARGATE ROAD, WESTWOOD, BROADSTAIRS, KENT CT10 2PR
TEL: 01843 861245 FAX: 01843 861245

Directions: From Canterbury take the A28 towards Margate, bearing right onto the A253 to Ramsgate. From Ramsgate take the A255 towards Broadstairs. The Star Inn can be found on the road which heads towards Margate.

Found in the Westwood area of Broadstairs, **The Star Inn** is an historic and interesting old inn that is well worth taking the trouble to visit. Dating back to the 18th century, the inn is thought to owe its name to its central position on the Isle of Thanet as this would have been where ancient cartographers placed their "star". Whether this

is true or not, the story has remained, as has the legend of the convivial evening spent here, in 1825, by the church wardens and choir of St Peter's church who came to dine here whilst beating the bounds of the parish. This was the first time the custom had been carried out since before the Napoleonic Wars

and the evening became so boisterous that the choir boys were thrown into a nearby pond. Whilst nothing quite as drastic as this happens here now, landlord Maurice Gleed does ensure that everyone enjoys their visit.

A popular and well-recommended establishment, this attractive inn is full of character, both inside and out. The freshly painted frontage leads to a cosy, distinctively decorated interior, which retains the original oak beams and wooden floor. A choice of real ales, plus all the usual beers, lagers and spirits, are served from the bar and there is also a tempting menu of food available each lunchtime. The dishes are simple and classic and provide excellent value for money.

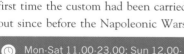

- ⏰ Mon-Sat 11.00-23.00; Sun 12.00-22.30
- 🍴 Good value, traditional fayre
- Ⓟ Beer garden, car park, children's play area
- 🎵 Regular live music
- @ mauricegleed@tiscali.co.uk
- ❓ Bleak House and Dickens House Museum 1 mile, Beach 1 mile, Margate 3 miles, RAF Manston Spitfire and Hurricane Memorial Building 4 miles

SUGAR LOAVES

56 EYHORNE STREET, HOLLINGBOURNE, KENT ME17 1TS
TEL: 01622 880220

Directions: From Maidstone, head east on the A20 for 4 miles. Just past the turning for the M20, turn left onto the B2163 and it is then just 1 mile to Hollingbourne.

The Sugar Loaves is a friendly traditional pub, situated in the heart of the village of Hollingbourne, and conveniently situated for both the M20 and the popular visitor attraction of Leeds Castle. The pub has a history going back to the 18th century, and today it retains a great deal of its charm. For the past seven years the pub has been run by Gary Whitcombe, and he has established it as a popular drinking place for locals and visitors alike. Gary is clearly full of good ideas and there always seems to be some activity going

on. There is an active golf society and there are regular themed nights or BBQs. You can ring or visit the website for full details of what events are coming up.

Home-cooked, traditional English dishes are served each lunchtime and in the evenings, Monday to Saturday. Sunday lunchtime offers traditional roasts. The menu offers a good selection to suit all tastes and appetites, all meals are freshly cooked to order and also provide excellent value for money. The bar stocks some real ales, including Master Brew, and a good selection of lagers and bottled beers. The interior is furnished with mainly church-pew style seating and drinks and food can be enjoyed throughout. There is a friendly, old-fashioned feel to the place that is clearly much loved by all who come here.

- 🕐 Mon-Thur & Sat 11.00-14.30, 18.00-23.00; Fri 11.00-15.00, 17.00-23.00; Sun 12.00-16.00, 19.00-22.30
- 🍴 Home-cooked, traditional English dishes
- £ Access, Mastercard, Visa, Delta, Switch, Electron, Solo
- Ⓟ Beer garden
- 🎵 Monthly quiz night, pool table
- @ e-mail: gary@sugarloaves.co.uk website: www.sugarloaves.co.uk
- ❓ Leeds Castle 1 mile, Stoneacre 3 miles, Kent County Showground 4 miles, Boughton Monchelsea Place 7 miles, Sittingbourne and Kemsley Light Railway 9 miles.

THE SWAN

THE STREET, GREAT CHART, NR. ASHFORD, KENT TN23 3AN
TEL: 01233 623250

> **Directions:** Leave the M20 at junction 9 and take the A28 road towards Tenterden. Just as you reach the outskirts of Ashford the village of Great Chart will be signposted to the right.

The Swan is a typical Kentish style building with a striking Dutch gable that ensures that anyone passing through Great Chart can't fail to notice it. Much loved by the locals and many visitors to the area, the current owners, Chris and Julie, have been here for six years and continue to ensure the pub's popularity. The emphasis is on providing relaxed surroundings in which everyone, young and old, can come and enjoy a drink, a tasty meal and to unwind. The relaxed atmosphere is only interrupted once a month when there is a karaoke night.

There is a large lawned area to the front of the pub and to the rear there is another small garden and plenty of car parking. Inside, this is a traditional and unspoilt inn that provides a comfortable environment in which to enjoy the welcoming hospitality. Low ceilings add to the intimacy around the open plan bar area and the comfortable leather armchairs and old pine furniture, suggest that this is just the place to linger for a while. As well as the excellent range of beers, lagers and real ales here there is an extensive menu of traditional English pub food available. From sandwiches through to the range of home-made pies – for which The Swan is famous - there is sure to be plenty to tickle the taste buds. Food is served both at lunchtimes and in the evenings Monday to Thursday, and all day Friday to Sunday.

- 🕐 Mon-Sat 11.30-23.00; Sun 12.00-22.30
- 🍴 Famed for serving a variety of delicious pies
- £ Visa, Access, Delta, Switch
- Ⓟ Beer garden, car park
- 🎵 Karaoke once a month
- ❓ International Station, Ashford 2 miles, Godinton Park 3 miles, Faggs Wood Forest Walk 7 miles, Swanton Mill 4 miles, Sissinghurst Castle Gardens 13 miles

THE SWAN

LONDON ROAD, TEYNHAM, SITTINGBOURNE, KENT ME9 9QH
TEL: 01795 521218

> **Directions:** From the M2 take junction 5 and follow the A249 towards Sheerness and turn right onto the A2 road through Sittingbourne. About 3 miles beyond the town is Teynham.

Dating from the 1930s, **The Swan** has been built in a mock-Tudor style with the upper storey being black and white timbered. Set slightly back from the busy main road, the pub is easily located in the centre of the village of Teynham, located midway between Sittingbourne and Faversham, in this remote part of Kent. Entering the pub, the open fires give out a warm welcome, and the simple décor is homely and comfortable. There are no pretensions here and the general air is

quite relaxed. Owned and run by Diane and Ian Huntley, the couple have been here five years and clearly love the place.

Diane is the cook, and responsible for the superb blackboard menus which offers plenty of choice. Whether you like a tasty steak, fish or a vegetarian meal there is sure to be something that will stimulate your appetite, and thankfully everything is sensibly priced too. Refreshingly, food is served all day until 8.30pm (no food on Monday except for Bank Holidays). Mostly frequented by locals, a friendly welcome is extended to one and all. You can try your hand at a game of darts and one Saturday each month there is live music. Please note the limited opening hours on Mondays.

- 🕐 Mon 16.00-20.00; Tues-Sat 12.00-23.00, Sun 12.00-22.30
- 🍽 Blackboard menu offering plenty of choice
- 🅿 Garden, car park
- 🎵 Live music one Saturday a month, darts
- ❓ Faversham 4 miles, Chilham Castle Gardens 9 miles, Canterbury 13 miles, Sittingbourne and Kemsley Light Railway 4 miles, South Swale Nature Reserve 3 miles

TUDOR ROSE

CHESTNUT STREET, BORDEN, SITTINGBOURNE, KENT ME9 8BT
TEL: 01795 842574 FAX: 01795 844552

Directions: Leaving the M2 at junction 5 take the A249 signposted for Sheerness. After a little over a mile, Borden will be signposted to the right.

The Tudor Rose is a large pub with restaurant that is well situated close to the A2 and the M2, not far from Sittingbourne. Dating back to the 1750s, this was originally two cottages which over

the years have been added to and extended, resulting in the impressive hostelry you see today. Neatly kept and well presented, the pub comes into its own in spring and summer when the outside is adorned with hanging baskets and flowering tubs.

Inside you will find a traditional bar

🕐 Mon-Sat 11.30-15.00, 18.00-23.00; Sun 12.00-15.00, 19.00-22.30

🍴 Traditional cuisine with carvery

💷 Visa, Mastercard, Delta, Switch

🅿 Car park, beer garden

❓ Sittingbourne and Kemsley Light Railway 3 miles, Kingshill Nature Reserve 8 miles, Kent County Showground 6 miles, Leeds Castle 8 miles, Boughton Monchelsea Place 13 miles

with, at the back, a conservatory restaurant area, while upstairs is a further restaurant which also serves as a function room. The Tudor Rose is well known for its superb, well-priced carvery. You can help yourself to as much as you can eat from the wide and tempting selection of starters and main courses - including a choice of salads, seafoods, four roasts, and fresh seasonal vegetables - followed by a choice of delectable desserts and coffee with fresh cream.

In addition there is also a menu of traditional English dishes, featuring fresh fish and other vegetarian options. Weather permitting, the charming, secluded garden is an ideal place to spend a long, warm summer evening with a drink.

Kent

THE TWO SAWYERS

WOOLAGE GREEN, CANTERBURY, KENT CT4 6SE
TEL: 01304 830295

Directions: From Canterbury pick up the A290, leading onto the A2 towards Dover. Just after the exit for the A260 there is a small turning on the right and in a mile you will come to Woolage Green.

Tucked away in the little village of Woolage Green, **The Two Sawyers** is really very well hidden. Most people would pass by on the A2 heading for Dover and wouldn't venture into these quiet country lanes where there are some real gems to be found. This is a particularly unspoilt example of an 18th-century village pub where time has almost stood still. Thankfully the new owners have ensured that everything is up to scratch for today's visitors, while retaining the charm and character.

The décor is homely and cosy with the bar area being dominated by a huge fireplace and the comfortable feel is

🕐 Mon-Sat 12.00-23.00; Sun 12.00-22.30

🍺 Available all day every day

Ⓟ Beer garden

🎵 Occasional live music

❓ Canterbury 8 miles, Howletts Zoo Park 6 miles, Kent Battle of Britain Museum 7 miles, Dover 9 miles, South Foreland Lighthouse 10 miles

continued through to the restaurant where there is seating for up to 28 diners. The food is traditional, home-cooked British fayre, just like your mother used to make, the servings are hearty and the prices reasonable too. It is refreshing to find somewhere that serves food all day every day, and here the selection of bar snacks and hot meals are available from midday until 10pm seven days a week. The location makes this an ideal eating place if you have just come off a ferry from the Continent and are heading home, or are simply exploring the area at leisure and have lost track of time. The landlord is very proud of his beers and there are usually a few fine examples worth sampling.

WALNUT TREE

FORGE LANE, EAST FARLEIGH, KENT ME15 0HJ
TEL: 01622 726368

Directions: East Farleigh lies just two miles southwest of Maidstone on the B2010.

The building, which now bears the name **The Walnut Tree**, was built in 1582 AD, during the reign of Elizabeth I, and started life as a farm dwelling on a large estate. The building eventually became a pub in 1784 and the name of The Walnut Tree was adopted in 1895. Today it is a perfect example of a traditional country pub, with all the character and atmosphere of over four centuries of history within its walls.

The Walnut Tree has ample car parking and also boasts a large garden to the rear with plenty of colourful planting, a pond and children's play equipment. For the amusement of the customers there are two Petanque pistes and a Bat 'n' Trap pitch.

Inside, the low beamed ceilings and tiled floors give the interior a cosy, homely feel and during the winter the open fires at each end of the building create an even more welcoming atmosphere. The bar offers a comprehensive range of Shepherd Neame Ales, including Spitfire and Master Brew, a fine selection of wines and spirits and a choice of soft drinks. Tea and coffee are also available all day. There is a comprehensive menu of hot and cold bar meals and snacks and a choice of home-made specials at realistic and competitive prices. All dishes are freshly prepared to order and use many locally sourced ingredients. Food is available at lunchtime and in the evenings (except Sunday and Monday nights).

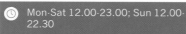

- Mon-Sat 12.00-23.00; Sun 12.00-22.30
- Delicious, home-cooked food
- Access, Mastercard, Visa, Delta
- Beer garden, children's play area
- Live music Thursday nights
- gdcross@hotmail.com
- Boughton Monchelsea Place 4 miles, Eyhorne Manor 5 miles, Leeds Castle 7 miles, Sissinghurst Place 13 miles, Kent County Showground 7 miles

THE WALNUT TREE

FORGE HILL, ALDINGTON, NR. ASHFORD, KENT TN25 7DT
TEL: 01233 720298

Directions: From the M20, close to Ashford, leave at junction 10 taking the A20 Folkestone road. After two and a half miles turn right onto the B2069, which takes you over the motorway, and the village of Aldington is just two miles

The Walnut Tree was built in the early 14th century and started life as no more than a timber-framed wattle and daub hut, not becoming an ale house until the 18th century, when the name was also adopted. During the Napoleonic Wars the village gained notoriety as the stronghold of the Aldington Gang, an infamous band of smugglers who roamed the marshes and shores of Kent, and the gang made the pub their headquarters, and a drop for illicit contraband. The pub has at least one ghost who makes his presence known on occasion, thought to be one of the smugglers, and during renovations of the kitchen a skeleton was discovered,

possibly a victim of the black death, which now thankfully has been laid to rest somewhere more suitable.

The food and drink served these days is of course totally legal, and although many visitors are drawn by the pub's history it is the fine ales and tasty food that keeps them coming back. The Walnut Tree has an excellent restaurant which serves fine food as well as bar meals and snacks, with the menu inspired by cuisine from all over the world, and the 'sizzling grill stones' are a speciality, where you can cook your own meat on hot stones at your table. The bar is well looked after by landlord Graham, and offers some popular Shepherd Neame real ales including Master Brew and Spitfire. The pub is located opposite the village cricket green, there is ample car parking space and a lovely beer garden.

- Mon-Sat 12.00-15.00, 18.30-23.00; Sun 12.00-22.30
- Bar food and a fine restaurant
- Visa, Mastercard, Delta, Switch
- Beer garden, children's play area, car park
- Charity events, race nights, darts, pool table, pub games
- Port Lympne Wild Animal Park 3 miles, Folkestone 11 miles, Romney, Hythe and Dymchurch Railway 6 miles, Folkestone Racecourse 6 miles

WESTBERE BUTTS

ISLAND ROAD, STURRY, CANTERBURY, KENT CT2 0EZ
TEL: 01227 712859 FAX: 01227 712859

Kent

> **Directions:** From the centre of Canterbury follow the A28 northeast towards Margate. After about three miles you will reach the Westbere Butts, located directly on the main road.

The Westbere Butts is conveniently located directly on the main road between Canterbury and Margate, making it an ideal stopping place for travellers, or anyone exploring this corner of Kent. A relatively modern pub, dating from the second World War, it conceals a most delightful beer garden which is well planted and features a large fish pond. The interior is bright and modern with a cosy public bar, well-furnished lounge bar and a beautiful conservatory restaurant which looks out onto the garden. There is a superb menu available all day, from 12 noon until 9pm, ranging from fresh fish and steaks to quick, light bar snacks, with the main dishes being changed regularly to make the most of seasonal produce. The pub is owned and personally run by Jason Bramley who is a young, laid-back and acute business man. He has created a friendly, efficiently-run establishment that is well liked by customers of all ages. Families are welcome and in fine weather the younger members can make use of the superb outdoor play area.

It is useful to know somewhere that can offer accommodation, and where could be more convenient than right here. There are five, well-appointed, spacious guest rooms all with en-suite facilities. The rooms are available all year round and the rates are reasonable. Simply ring for full details and availability.

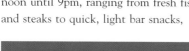

- 🕐 Mon-Sat 11.00-23.00; Sun 12.00-22.30
- 🍴 Food available all day every day
- 💷 Visa, Mastercard, Delta, Switch
- 🛏 Five en-suite rooms
- 🅿 Beer garden, children's play area
- @ Jason@jdbramley.freeserve.co.uk
- ❓ Canterbury 3 miles, Howletts Zoo Park 4 miles, Herne Bay 6 miles, Deal Castle 16 miles, Margate 12 miles, Dickens House Museum and Bleak House 15 miles

THE WHEATSHEAF

HIGH STREET, KEMSING, SEVENOAKS, KENT TN15 6NA
TEL: 01732 761038

Directions: From Sevenoaks follow the A25 east towards Maidstone. At Seal, just over a mile, turn left, crossing over the motorway, and then take the first right where The Wheatsheaf can be found in the heart of Kemsing.

At the heart of the ancient village of Kemsing visitors will find the historic St Edith's Well, named after the daughter of the Saxon King Edgar. Here you will also find a watering hole of another kind, **The Wheatsheaf** public house. Dating back to the 1700s, the building retains much of its original character and remains totally unspoilt. Inside there is a cosy bar and lounge area both of which feature oak beamed ceilings and a welcoming atmosphere, enjoyed by a wide variety of clientele. In addition there is a large restaurant, seating over 50 diners, where a delicious range of meals is available. The menu, which is changed weekly to make the most of seasonal produce, features homemade, traditional dishes including fish and steaks. Everything is sensibly priced and served in good portions.

Your hosts are Dave and Alison Dockree, and the couple have been at the Wheatsheaf for two years, firmly establishing it as a gathering place for the local community as well as attracting visitors to the area. A lively and popular inn, there is monthly pub quiz and live music every other week. Ring for details.

- 🕐 Mon-Sat 12.00-23.00; Sun 12.00-22.30
- 🍴 Large, luxurious restaurant
- 💷 Access, Mastercard, Visa, Delta
- 🅿 Car parking, beer garden, patio
- 🎵 Monthly quiz, live music alternate weekends, satellite TV, cribbage, darts
- @ davedockree@hotmail.com
- ❓ St Edith's Well, Sevenoaks 3 miles, Knole 4 miles, Ightham Mote 4 miles, Emmetts Garden 7 miles, Chartwell 9 miles, Brands Hatch 4 miles

WHEATSHEAF INN

MAIN ROAD, MARSH GREEN, EDENBRIDGE, KENT TN8 5QL
TEL: 01732 864091

Directions: From Royal Tunbridge Wells, take the A264 East Grinstead road due west. After 7 miles turn right onto the B2026. After just over four miles the B2028 is signed on the left, and this will lead you to Marsh Green.

The Wheatsheaf is a traditional roadside inn, which can be found in the heart of the small village of Marsh Green. It is an attractive building, which in summer months is adorned with colourful hanging baskets and flowering tubs. Much loved by locals, and attracting customers from the nearby towns, it has been run by Neil Foster for over ten years. Well known for the superb range of excellent real ales, there are usually nine available at any one

time, all constantly changing. In fact, the superb quality of the ales has been recognised by CAMRA, with the Wheatsheaf being the 2002 West Kent winner.

To complement the well stocked bar, there is good menu of home-cooked traditional English dishes, served in good-sized portions. There is a separate, attractive conservatory restaurant, though meals can also be taken in the bar, and food is served at lunchtime and in the evening, seven days a week. Marsh Green is a pretty village and there are some nice local walks in the surrounding countryside to work off your lunch, or help build up an appetite.

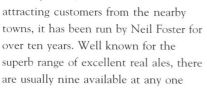

- 🕐 Mon-Sat 11.00-23.00; Sun 12.00-22.30
- 🍴 Superb home-cooked food
- 💷 Access, Mastercard, Visa, Delta
- 🅿 Beer garden, al fresco dining, BBQ
- 🎵 Occasional quiz nights
- @ fosterinn@aol.com
- ❓ Lingfield Park Racecourse 3 miles, Starborough Castle, Haxted Mill 2 miles, Hever Castle 3 miles, Greathed Manor 2 miles, Chartwell 5 miles

THE WHITE HORSE INN

53 HIGH STREET, BRIDGE, CANTERBURY, KENT CT4 5LA
TEL: 01227 830249 FAX: 01227 832814

Directions: Follow the signs to Dover. Where the road meets the A2 (Canterbury by-pass) then follow the signs Bridge into village. The White Horse Inn is in the centre of the village with good parking facilities.

Here is the small village of Bridge, Alan Walton and his family have created one of the nicest pubs in the whole of Kent. Located at a river crossing this is obviously the source of the village's name. Until recent times, it continued to be a busy thoroughfare but thankfully, since the A2 by-pass was opened in 1976, it has become much quieter.

The superb **White Horse Inn** is a large hostelry with origins in the 15th century and the whole building has retained much of its historic character. The exterior is beautifully maintained and decorated for most of the year with colourful hanging baskets and flowering tubs.

Inside, the traditional feel is continued with attractive leather chairs, woodblock floor and wooden furnishings, with feature fireplaces in the bars. Food is served each lunchtime and every evening except Sunday.

The superb food is enjoyed by the most discerning of diners, with regular customers travelling from all over this part of Kent and the menus offer the best of traditional local cuisine with French, Italian and Asian overtones. The classically-trained chef is Alan's son, and together they have created a superb pub with a well-deserved reputation.

- Mon-Sat 11.00-15.00, 18.00-23.00; Sun 12.00-16.00, Closed Sunday evenings
- Superb menus with French, Italian and Asian themes
- Visa, Mastercard, Delta, Switch
- Occasional live jazz
- thewaltons_thewhitehorse@hotmail.com
- Canterbury 3 miles, Howletts Zoo Park 1 mile, Chilham Castle Gardens 6 miles, Herne Bay 11 miles, Druidstone Wildlife Park 6 miles

THE WHITE HORSE INN

105 MAIN ROAD, SUNDRIDGE, NR. SEVENOAKS, KENT TN14 6EH
TEL/FAX: 01959 562837

Directions: If you are travelling around the M25 in an anti-clockwise direction, leave at junction 6 and follow the A25 towards Westerham and onto Sevenoaks. Sundridge can be found midway between the two.

Located directly on the A25 Westerham road, **The White Horse Inn** can be easily located in the heart of Sundridge, right on the traffic lights, and if you are travelling here by car there is plenty of parking to be found one side. Open all day every day, this is a genuine 17th-

century former coaching inn which has a traditional look and feel. Extended in the early 1900s, the white-washed frontage is adorned with hanging baskets all year round, giving a splash of colour.

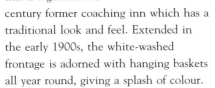

🕐 Mon-Sat 12.00-23.00; Sun 12.00-22.30

🍴 Good, fresh food offering good value

£ Visa, Mastercard, Delta, Switch, Amex

Ⓟ Beer garden, car park

🎵 Fortnightly karaoke, live music Saturday nights, pool table

❓ Knole Park and House 5 miles, Chartwell 4 miles, Emmetts Gardens 2 miles, Quebec House 2 miles, Hever Castle 8 miles, Ightham Mote 8 miles, Biggin Hill Airfield 8 miles

Inside, the décor has a comfortable, lived in feel, with the original low ceilings, oak beams and big open fires adding to the character. All kept spotlessly clean throughout, the relaxed surroundings are much loved by the owner Jeremy and Maria, and are here to stay. There are absolutely no plans for introducing a modern, minimal décor in the near future! Appealing to a wide ranging local clientele, one of the popular features is the good value, fresh food that is available lunchtime and in the evening Monday to Saturday. On Sundays a traditional roast is served until 4pm. Everything is prepared to order using good quality, fresh ingredients, and offers good value for money.

WHITE HORSE INN

7 CANTERBURY ROAD, HAWKINGE, NR. FOLKESTONE,
KENT CT18 7BW   TEL: 01303 892268 FAX: 01303 891686

Directions: From junction 12 on the M20 pick up the A20 towards Dover and after barely a mile turn left on to the A260. The White Horse Inn lies approximately a mile and a half along this road.

Conveniently located close to the main cross Channel ports of Folkestone and Dover, **The White Horse Inn** is a charming old inn that lies somewhat off the beaten track, enjoying the quiet and pleasant surroundings of the North Downs. Dating back to 1802, this attractive Georgian building once hosted cockfights in its upper rooms but that violent sport has been replaced by the more sedate pub games of darts, pool and cribbage. A warm and cosy place during the winter, those visiting the inn in the summer months can make use of The White Horse's large and secluded beer garden that is ideal for adults wishing to soak up the sunshine and for children to play in the fresh air.

Very much a locals' inn, landlords Angela and Ron have created a relaxed and informal environment that is a popular meeting place and also where visitors can be sure of a friendly welcome. Well known for its well-stocked bar, this free house offers several real ales and some fine lagers as well as all the other beers, ciders and spirits. A tasty selection of simple pub fayre is offered at lunchtime between midday and 2pm with everything home-cooked and freshly prepared to order. Ron is the chef, and in summer he has been known to venture outside and prepare a barbeque. The White Horse Inn is a friendly place, offering charming country hospitality.

- Mon-Sat 11.00-23.00; Sun 12.00-22.30
- Bar meals and snacks lunchtime only
- Visa, Mastercard, Delta, Switch, Amex, Diners.
- Beer garden, car park
- Occasional live music, quiz nights, pool, darts, bar games
- ron@wraight933.freeserve.co.uk
- Kent Battle of Britain Museum, Folkestone 2 miles, Beach 2 miles, Channel Tunnel Terminal 3 miles, St Radigund's Abbey 4 miles, Hythe 5 miles, Dover 6 miles

THE WINDMILL

EYHORNE STREET, HOLLINGBOURNE, KENT ME17 1TR
TEL: 01622 880280 FAX: 01622 880280

> **Directions:** Turning off the M20 at junction 8 follow signs to Leeds Castle. At the roundabout Hollingbourne is signposted along the B2163 to the left.

The Windmill can be found at the lower end of the village of Hollingbourne close to the post office and village hall. This 16th-century, former coaching inn has the genuine feel of an old country pub housed within a beautiful old building of a traditional style, adorned with colourful hanging baskets. It is a substantial size for such a small village and enjoys such a fine reputation that the regular clientele are attracted from all over north Kent.

Inside, the rural feel is continued with stone and brick flooring, wooden beamed ceilings and open fires. The bar areas are also well divided into cosy nooks and crannies, so you can be sure of enjoying a quiet drink, undisturbed by your neighbours. There is a children's play area, for keeping the younger visitors occupied, and outside you will also find a large beer garden and patio area, ideal for al fresco dining when the weather allows.

The Windmill serves a full and varied menu offering a superlative choice of dishes, ranging from fresh fish to huge steaks. Everything is of the highest quality, using the finest ingredients and freshly prepared to order. Food is served each weekday lunchtime and evening and all day Saturday and Sunday.

There is a separate, non-smoking area. The Windmill gets busy in the evenings and at weekends, so you'd be wise to book in advance. The bar is equally well stocked with an excellent selection of real cask ales kept on tap. Highly recommended.

- 🕐 Mon-Fri 11.00-15.00, 17.00-23.00; Sat 11.00-23.00; Sun 12.00-22.30
- 🍴 Superb menu offering plenty of variety
- 💷 Visa, Mastercard, Delta, Switch
- 🅿 Beer garden, car park, children's play area
- @ thewindmillpub@aol.com
- ❓ Eyhorne Manor, Leeds Castle 1 mile, Stoneacre 3 miles, Boughton Monchelsea Place 7 miles, Kent County Showground 4 miles, Sittingbourne and Kemsley Light Railway 9 miles

Please note all cross references refer to page numbers

SUSSEX

East Sussex was the location of some of the most famous events in the history of England. The coastal village of Pevensey was the landing place of William, Duke of Normandy and his army in 1066 and, as every school child knows, William proceeded to defeat Harold near Hastings and claim the crown of England. Hastings and Battle, the town that grew up around the site of the battlefield, have museums and exhibitions on these momentous historical events. The victorious Normans soon set about building castles and fortifications from which to defend their new territory, along with religious buildings, and the area is still rich in Norman architecture.

The south coast was always susceptible to invasion and, in the days before the Royal Navy, the confederation of Cinque Ports was established to provide a fleet of ships to defend the coast. Many Sussex towns, now some distance from the sea, were part of the confederation. The silting up of the harbours has changed the landscape of the East Sussex coast considerably in the last 1,000 years.

Nowadays the coast is the preserve of holidaymakers, taking advantage of the usually moderate climate and the bracing sea air. The thriving resorts of Brighton and Eastbourne began life as quiet fishing villages but

PLACES OF INTEREST

developed rapidly at the beginning of the 19th century. Brighton is best known for its exotic Royal Pavilion, designed by John Nash for the Prince Regent, in magnificent Indian style, with minarets and domes. Eastbourne, by contrast, was carefully planned and laid out in

Petworth House

genteel style by William Cavendish, the 7th Duke of Devonshire, close to the chalk cliffs of Beachy Head. St Leonards and Bexhill are quieter resorts and perhaps the most picturesque of them all is Rye, with its many medieval buildings.

Away from the coast, on the high ridges of the Weald, is the largest area in southeast England that has never been ploughed and put to agricultural use. Ashdown Forest was a royal hunting ground and its thriving population of deer made it a favourite sporting place. The network of tracks across the forest goes back to prehistoric times, the Romans built a road straight across it and the rights of commoners to gather wood for fuel, cut peat and graze cattle, were well established by Norman times. Although much of the woodland has been lost as fuel and for shipbuilding over the centuries, the remaining forest is protected as an Area of Outstanding Natural Beauty and Site of Special Scientific Interest. The surrounding area is characterised by small towns and villages of weather boarded cottages, traditional hall houses and unspoilt farmsteads.

Many artists and writers of the 19th and 20th centuries chose to live here. AA Milne set the *Winnie the Pooh* stories in Ashdown Forest and surrounding area. Virginia Woolf and her husband Leonard lived at Monk's House, Rodmell, while her sister, Vanessa Bell, was at nearby Charleston Farmhouse, in Selmeston. The Elms at Rottingdean was the home of Rudyard Kipling until 1902, when he moved to Burwash, and the village of Ditchling was home to several artists and crafts people at the centre of the Arts and Crafts Movement.

Despite being home to an international airport at Gatwick, which is a transport hub for road and rail as well as air travel, West Sussex remains an essentially rural landscape dominated by the South Downs, a magnificent range of chalk hills. The South Downs Way, a 100 mile bridleway along the crest of the hills from Winchester to Beachy Head, has panoramic views across the Weald to the north and south to the sea. It traces the long history of this area along ancient trails, passing Bronze Age barrows and Iron Age hill forts. On the coast, Chichester, the county town, once a busy haunt of smugglers, is now a thriving sailing centre, while the small fishing villages of the past are quiet holiday resorts like Littlehampton, Bognor Regis and Worthing. The ancient woodland of the West Sussex Weald is now a landscape of pastures and hedgerows and small country villages. The trees were felled for fuel to drive the furnaces of the iron industry, which flourished here for centuries. The legacy of this prosperous industry can be seen in the wealth of elaborate buildings, particularly churches, built on the profits.

Evidence of human habitation and culture abound in this area. The Romans settled in Chichester in the 1st century, and it later became a great medieval religious centre with a fine Norman cathedral. At Fishbourne, the Roman remains of a splendid palace built for the Celtic King Cogidubnus, were discovered in 1960. At Arundel, the original Norman motte and double bailey design of its magnificent castle is still visible as well as the alterations and additions of subsequent generations. Norman churches are everywhere,

Brighton Beach

often little altered over the centuries. In the tiny village of Sompting, there is a Saxon church with a pyramid capped tower, unique in England. Near Ardingly, Wakehurst Place is the striking

Elizabethan mansion of the Culpeper family, with a magnificent collection of trees and shrubs. Wakehurst Place is also home to the Millennium Seed Bank, a project, which aims to ensure

Bodiam Castle

the continued survival of over 24,000 plant species worldwide. Petworth House is an elegant late 17th century building, reminiscent of a French château with a garden landscaped by Capability Brown. Close to East Grinstead, the remarkable Victorian country house, Standen, has been sensitively restored to its original Arts and Crafts Movement style.

Many great artists and literary figures have found this region inspirational. Turner loved to paint its landscapes and harbours. HG Wells, Anthony Trollope and Tennyson all lived here. The composer Edward Elgar wrote his famous cello concerto at Fittleworth in 1917. And at Hurstpierpoint, at the Elizabeth mansion, Danny, Lloyd George and his war cabinet drew up the terms of the armistice, which ended World War I.

Within easy reach of London by rail or road but not so near as to suffer too much from commuter belt blight, served by an international airport and close to channel ports for travel to the continent, it is no surprise that many notable people continue to make their homes here. Few places so elegantly combine 21st century convenience with the unspoiled charm of a rich historic heritage.

Alfriston

Alfriston is one of the oldest
and best preserved villages in
Sussex. The old market cross
still stands in the square, one
of two left in the county (the
other is in Chichester). One
of the oldest buildings
remaining in the town is the
Star Inn, built in the early
15th century as a resting place

Alfriston Market Cross

for pilgrims on their way to and from the
shrine of St Richard at Chichester. The
former prosperity of this town is reflected
in its splendid 14th century parish
church that is often referred to as **The
Cathedral of the Downs**. Beside the
church is the thatched and timbered
Clergy House, the first building to be
acquired - for £10 - by the National
Trust, in 1896. To the north of the
village lies **Drusillas Park**, a child
friendly zoo with a play area, a train ride
and attractive gardens.

Amberley

An attractive village of thatched
cottages situated above the River Arun,
Amberley is an ancient place whose
name means 'fields yellow with butter-
cups'. The village church is thought to
stand on the foundations of a Saxon
building constructed by St Wilfrid, the
missionary who converted the South
Saxons to Christianity. During the late
14th century, when there was a large
threat of a French sea invasion, Bishop
Rede of Chichester enlarged the summer

palace built for the bishops and added a
great curtain wall. Still more a manor
house than a true castle, **Amberley
Castle** is said to have offered protection
to Charles II during his flight to France
in 1651. Today, it is a privately owned
luxury hotel.

Situated just to the south of Amberley
and on the site of an old chalk pit and
limeworks is **Amberley Museum**, a
working museum that concentrates on
the industry of this area.

Ardingly

Ardingly is chiefly famous for being the
home of the showground for the South of
England Agricultural Society. Although
there is some modern building, the old
part of the village has remained fairly
unspoilt. To the west of the village, a
tributary of the River Ouse has been
dammed to form **Ardingly Reservoir**, a
200 acre lake which offers some excellent fishing as well as waterside walks
and a nature trail. Just north of Ardingly,
at the top end of the reservoir, lies
Wakehurst Place, the Tudor home of the

Wakehurst Place

despite several alterations and rebuildings, remains clearly visible today. The second largest castle in England, it has been the seat of the Dukes of Norfolk and the Earls of Arun for over 700 years.

Ashdown Forest

This ancient tract of sandy heathland and woodland on the high ridges of the Weald is designated an Area of Outstanding Natural Beauty, a Site of Special Scientific Interest and a Special Protection Area for birds. It is a place of recreation with many picnic areas and scenic viewpoints and open access for walking throughout. The deer have returned and the clumps of Scotch pines that make prominent landmarks on the higher points of the forest were planted in the 19th century.

Culpeper family, who arrived here in the 15th century. Over the years, but particularly during the 20th century, the owners of Wakehurst Place have built up a splendid collection of trees and shrubs in the natural dramatic landscapes of woodlands, valleys and lakes. Now leased to the Royal Botanic Gardens at Kew, the 500 acre gardens are open to the public throughout the year. Wakehurst Place is also home to the **Millennium Seed Bank**, a project which aims to ensure the continued survival of over 24,000 plant species world-wide.

Arundel

A settlement since before the Romans invaded, this quiet and peaceful town, which lies beneath the battlements of one of the most impressive castles in the country, is a strategically important site where the major east-west route through Sussex crosses the River Arun. With a similar plan to that of Windsor castle, **Arundel Castle** consisted of a motte with a double bailey, a design which,

Battle

This historic settlement is, of course, renowned as being the site of the momentous battle, on 14th October 1066, between the armies of Harold, Saxon King of England, and William, Duke of Normandy. The Battle of Hastings was a particularly gruesome affair, even for those times, and it was not until late in the afternoon that Harold finally fell on the field. After his victory, William set about fulfilling his vow that, if he was victorious, he would

Battle Abbey

anniversary of this first race is celebrated each year in May with the **Bexhill Festival of Motoring**.

Bodiam

Situated in the valley of the River Rother, this attractive village is home to one of the most romantic castles in the country. Construction on **Bodiam Castle** was begun in 1385 when the technology of castle building was at its peak and before the use of gunpowder. Completely surrounded by a wide moat, the arrow slits, cannon ports and aptly named murder holes (through which objects were thrown at attackers below) were never used in anger. However, there was a minor skirmish here in 1484 and, during the Civil War, the castle surrendered without a shot being fired.

build an abbey. Choosing the very spot where Harold fell, **Battle Abbey** was begun straight away and was consecrated in 1094. Although little of the early Norman features remain, Battle Abbey has much to offer the visitor.

Bexhill-on-Sea

This small seaside resort was founded in the 1880s by the influential De La Warr family, who lived at the original village of Bexhill, a mile from the coast. Among the landmarks on the promenade, the **De La Warr Pavilion** stands out. Built in the 1930s by Erich Mendelsohn and Serge Chermayeff, it is a fine and an early example of the functional style of architecture that was becoming fashionable at the time. Looking rather like an ocean going liner, with its welded steel frame, curves, abundance of glass and terraces, the Grade I listed building is now a renowned centre for arts and culture. In 1902 the town witnessed the birth of British motor racing when a race and other speed trials were held here; the

Bognor Regis

Towards the end of the 18th century Sir Richard Hotham, a wealthy London milliner, sought to transform Bognor from a quiet fishing village into a fashionable resort to rival Brighton. He set about constructing some imposing residences, including The Dome in Upper Bognor Road, and even planned to have the town renamed Hothampton. Unfortunately, the fashionable set of the day stayed away and Hotham's dream was never realised - at least not in his lifetime. In 1929, George V came to the resort to convalesce following a serious illness and, on the strength of his stay, the town was granted the title Regis. The resort is known for its 'Birdmen', and the annual international **Birdman Rally** held in August draws huge crowds. The competitors, in a variety of classes, take it in turns to hurl themselves off the pier in an attempt to make the longest un-powered flight and so win the coveted competition.

Bosham

It was here, on the shore, that King Canute is said to have ordered back the waves in an attempt to demonstrate his kingly powers. It was an important port from the Middle Ages and is now a place for keen yachtsmen as well as a charming place to explore. The narrow streets that lead down to the harbour are filled with elegant 17th and 18th century flint and brick buildings amongst which is the **Bosham Walk Craft Centre**. This fascinating collection of little shops selling all manner of arts, crafts, fashions and antiques within a old courtyard setting, also holds craft demonstrations and exhibitions throughout the season.

Bramber

The name Bramber is derived from the Saxon 'Brymmburh' meaning fortified hill, and when William de Braose built

his castle it was probably on the founda-tions of a previous Saxon stronghold. Completed in 1090, **Bramber Castle** comprised a gatehouse and a number of domestic buildings surrounded by a curtain wall. An important stronghold whilst Bramber was still a port, the castle did not survive the Civil War. Today, the stark ruins can be seen on the hilltop.

During the 15th century, the lands of the de Braose family were transferred to William Waynflete, the then Bishop of Winchester and founder of Magdalen College, Oxford. It was Waynflete who was responsible for constructing **St Mary's House**, in 1470, a striking medieval residence with fine wood-panelled rooms, Elizabethan trompe l'œil paintings and medieval shuttered windows.

Brighton

By the time of the Prince Regent's first visit to the village, at 21 years of age in 1783, Brighton was already becoming a popular place but still remained concen-trated around the old village of Brighthelmstone. The Prince Regent,

St Mary's House

later to become George IV, was so taken with the resort that he first took a house here and then built his famous **Royal Pavilion** in the resort. The small farmhouse on the site was transformed in 1787 by architect Henry Holland into a neoclassical building with a dome and rotunda. Finally between 1815 and 1822, the pavilion seen today was

Bateman's

created in a magnificent Indian style, by John Nash. Based on a maharajah's palace, complete with minarets, onion shaped domes and pinnacles, the Royal Pavilion has been the most well-known Brighton landmark for almost 200 years.

For many visitors to Brighton a visit to **The Lanes**, the warren of narrow streets that represent what is left of the old village, is a must. Today, these tiny alleys are the preserve of smart boutiques, antique shops and restaurants.

The best-known features on the seafront are the **Palace Pier** and the Volk's railway, the first electric railway in the country.

Burwash

Burwash was, between the 15th and 17th centuries, a major centre of the Wealden iron industry, which brought much prosperity to the village.

However, it is not the village that brings most people to Burwash, though it certainly deserves attention, but a house just outside. In 1902, Rudyard Kipling moved from Rottingdean to **Bateman's**

to combat the growing problem of over-enthusiastic sightseers. Located down a steep and narrow lane, the Jacobean house was originally built in 1634 for a prosperous local ironmaster. With its surrounding 33 acres of beautiful grounds, landscaped by Kipling and his wife, it proved the perfect retreat.

Buxted

This village has long been dominated by the great house of **Buxted Park**. This Grade II listed building was built along classical lines in 1725. Almost destroyed by fire in 1940, it was restored by architect Basil Ionides. Although altered from its original design, it was sensitively rebuilt using numerous period pieces from other locations. There are doors and chimney pieces by Robert Adam, cabinets and pillars from grand London houses and country mansions and a particularly fine staircase from a house in Old Burlington Street in London. It is now a hotel and the 312 acres of gardens and parkland are open to visitors taking afternoon teas.

Camber

Camber Castle is a fine example of a the coastal defences built by Henry VIII in the 16th century. The fortress seems rather far inland today but when it was built it held a commanding position on a spit of land on one side of the Rother estuary. Now in the hands of English Heritage, the castle is open on a limited basis.

Chichester

The invading Roman legions used the town as a base camp, and both the city walls and the four major thoroughfares follow the original Roman town plan. They cross at the point where the fine **Butter Cross** now stands, an ornate structure built in 1500 by Bishop Edward

Chichester Cathedral

Story to provide shelter for the many traders who came to sell their wares at the busy market. Lying in the heart of the city, **Chichester Cathedral**, a centre for Christian worship for over 900 years, is unique on two counts. It is the only medieval English cathedral that can be seen from the sea rather than being secluded by its own close, and it has a detached belfry. Among the treasures within the cathedral are the shrine of St Richard of Chichester, some fine Norman arches, a set of 14th century choir stalls and some excellent modern works of art. There is an altar tapestry by John Piper, a stained glass window by Marc Chagall and a painting by Graham Sutherland of Christ appearing to Mary Magdalene. However, the most important treasures to be seen are the Norman sculptures: *The Raising of Lazarus* and *Christ Arriving in Bethany*, which can be found on the south wall.

One of the city's most distinctive modern buildings can be found at Oaklands Park, close by the city walls. The **Chichester Festival Theatre** was opened in 1962 and this splendid hexagonal building has since gained a reputation for staging the finest classical and contemporary drama, opera and ballet. For those with other interests, the **Mechanical Music and Doll Collection** offers a fascinating tour through the last 100 years of mechanical music. The **Royal Military Police Museum** is housed in the Keep at Roussillon Barracks and is a must for anyone interested in military history.

Cootham

The village is synonymous with **Parham**, the grandest of the Elizabethan mansions that were built below the northern slopes of the Downs. The splendid Elizabethan interiors have been restored to their former glory, including the magnificent 160 foot Long Gallery, Great Hall and Great Parlour, and an exceptional collection of period furniture, oriental carpets, rare needlework and fine paintings are on show. The gardens too have been restored and the seven acres of wooded parkland contain a walled garden with herb beds and a Wendy House, greenhouses where plants and flowers are grown for the house, a lake and a statue garden.

Cuckfield

Before the new turnpike road was built in 1807, Cuckfield stood on the main route from London to the south coast and, because of this, it became a busy staging post. George IV used to stop here on his way to Brighton. A horse-drawn coach service was maintained from here by an American right up until the beginning of World War I when the horses were needed for the war effort.

To the north lie **Borde Hill Gardens**, a splendid typically English garden of special botanical interest in some 200 acres of spectacular Sussex parkland and woods.

East Dean

This charming village at the foot of the South Downs is one of the county's most picturesque, with a village green surrounded by flint cottages, a pub and an ancient church. Just south of the village, right on the coast, is **Birling Gap**, a huge cleft in the cliffs which offers the only access to the beach between Eastbourne and Cuckmere Haven. To the east of the gap lie the **Seven Sisters**, huge great blocks of chalk that guard the coast between Eastbourne and Seaford.

East Grinstead

Situated 400 feet above sea level on a sandstone hill, East Grinstead has a rich history that dates back to the early 13th century. The **Town Museum**, housed in East Court, is a fine building that was originally constructed as a private residence in 1769; the Greenwich Meridian passes through the town at this point.

Borde Hill Gardens

To the south of East Grinstead lies **Standen**, a remarkable late Victorian country mansion that is a showpiece of the Arts and Crafts Movement. Completed in 1894 by Philip Webb, an associate of William Morris, for a prosperous London solicitor, the house was constructed using a variety of traditional local building materials. Morris designed the internal furnishings such as the carpets, wallpapers and textiles. Now fully restored, the house, owned by the National Trust, can be seen in all its 1920s splendour, including details such as original electric light fittings. From near Standen runs the **Bluebell Railway**, which offers a pleasant journey by steam train through the Sussex Weald to Sheffield Park, the railway's headquarters, via the 1930s station at Horsted Keynes.

Eastbourne

When George III sent his children here in the summer of 1780, it was, in fact, two villages, the larger of which lay a mile inland from the coast. Slowly the villages were developed and merged but it was William Cavendish, later the 7th Duke of Devonshire, who really instigated Eastbourne's rapid growth as a seaside resort from the 1850s onwards. Among the first buildings that Cavendish had constructed are the handsome Regency style Burlington Hotel, St Saviour's Church,

the Town Hall and the extremely elegant railway station. The classic pier was built in the 1880s.

In the centre of Eastbourne is the **Museum of Shops** with its Victorian streets, room-settings and displays depicting shopping and social history over the last 100 years. As a coastal town, during the scare of French invasions at the beginning of the 19th century, Eastbourne had its own defences. The **Martello Tower No 73**, one of 103 built along the south coast, is today home to a small **Puppet Museum**. Another Napoleonic defence, the **Redoubt Fortress**, houses the **Military Museum of Sussex**.

The sea has always played an important part in the life of the town, and in the **RNLI Lifeboat Museum** the history of the town's lifeboats is charted through a series of interesting exhibits. Nearby **Beachy Head** is one of the most spectacular chalk precipices in England, with a sheer drop of over 500 feet in places. On the clifftop is the **Beachy Head Countryside Centre** which focuses on

Beachy Head

downland life and includes numerous wildlife displays. This is also the end (or the beginning) of the **South Downs Way**, a long distance bridleway that was established in 1972.

Findon

An attractive village whose main square is surrounded by some elegant 18th century houses. Situated within the South Downs Area of Outstanding Natural Beauty, Findon is famous for being the venue of one of the two great Sussex sheep fairs - the other is at Lewes. Markets have been held on Nepcote Green since the 13th century and the Findon **Sheep Fair** has been an annual event each September since the 18th century. From Findon there is easy access to **Cissbury Ring**, the largest Iron Age hillfort on the South Downs.

Fishbourne

This village is known to the world by the splendid Roman remains discovered in 1960. **Fishbourne Roman Palace** was built around AD 75 for the Celtic King Cogidubnus, who collaborated with the Roman conquerors. His reward was this magnificent palace with underfloor heating, hot baths, a colonnade, an ornamental courtyard garden and lavish decorations. Among the superb remains are a garden and numerous

mosaic floors, including the famous **Cupid on a Dolphin** mosaic.

Glyndebourne

Glyndebourne, a part Tudor, part Victorian country house, just a mile north of Glynde village, is now the home of the world famous **Glyndebourne Opera House**. In the early 1930s, John Christie, a school master, music lover and inheritor of the house, married the accomplished opera singer Audrey Mildmay and, as regular visitors to European music festivals, they decided to bring opera to England and their friends. In the idyllic setting of their country estate, they built a modest theatre and, in 1934, Glyndebourne first opened with a performance of Mozart's *Marriage of Figaro*.

Goodwood

Goodwood House is the spectacular country home of the Dukes of Richmond. It was first acquired by the 1st Duke of Richmond (the natural son of

Goodwood House

Charles II and his beautiful French mistress, Louise de Keroualle) in 1697 so that he could ride with the local hunt. The original, modest hunting lodge still remains in the grounds, but has been superseded by the present mansion, built on a grand scale in the late 18th century for the 3rd Duke by the architect James Wyatt. At the same time the splendid stables were added. Now refurbished by the Earl and Countess of March, several rooms in this impressive house, including the state apartments, are open to visitors. The house is the focal point of the Goodwood Estate, some 12,000 acres of downland which also incorporate the world famous **Goodwood Racecourse**. Racing has taken place here for nearly 200 years with the five-day summer meeting ('Glorious Goodwood') the highlight of the season.

Nymans

Groombridge

Centred around a triangular green are attractive 15th and 16th century estate cottages and a superb manor house **Groombridge Place**, dating from the 17th century. Set within terraced gardens, it has a small museum dedicated to Sir Arthur Conan Doyle, who was a frequent visitor to the house and the surrounding woodland, dubbed the Enchanted Forest. This is indeed a magical place, with a wild wood area, a Celtic Forest, a North American Wood and a Jurassic Valley. The gardens and woodlands are open throughout the summer.

Handcross

Close to this little village, which stood on the old London to Brighton road, are two glorious gardens. To the southeast lie the superb National Trust owned gardens of **Nymans**. At the heart of Nymans is the round walled garden, created with the help of the late 19th century gardening revivalists William Robinson and Gertrude Jekyll. Elsewhere, the gardens are laid out in a series of 'rooms', where visitors can walk from garden to garden taking in the old roses, the topiary, the laurel walk and the sunken garden. Just northeast of Handcross is another smaller, though not less glorious garden, **High Beeches Gardens**. Here, in the enchanting woodlands and water gardens, is a collection of rare and exotic plants as well as native wild flowers in a natural meadow setting.

Hastings

Long before William the Conqueror made his landing on the beaches of nearby Pevensey, Hastings was the principal town of a small Saxon province that straddled the county border between Sussex and Kent. Following the Battle of Hastings, which actually took place six miles away at Battle, the victorious William returned to Hastings where the Normans began to build their first stone castle in England. Choosing the high ground of West Hill as their site, the massive structure is now in ruins and all that can be seen on the cliff top are the original motte and parts of the curtain wall. However, there are commanding views from here and also the permanent display - **1066 Story at Hastings Castle**. Housed in a medieval siege tent, the exhibition transports visitors back to October 1066, through clever use of audio-visual techniques.

After the Conquest, this already important port became a leading Cinque Port, a role it played until the harbour began to silt up in Elizabethan times. Nevertheless, the fishing industry has managed to survive and today fishing vessels continue to be hoisted on to the shingle beach by a winch. The old fishermen's church of St Nicholas is now home to the **Fishermen's Museum**, which has, as its centrepiece, *The Enterprise*, one of the last of Hastings' sailing luggers. Staying with a maritime theme, the **Shipwreck Heritage Centre** is an award winning museum that is devoted to the history of wrecked ships.

The old part of Hastings consists of a network of narrow streets and alleyways - or 'twittens' - which lie between West and East Hill. There are two cliff railways, one running up each of the hills. West Hill railway runs underground taking passengers to Hastings Castle and St Clement's Caves whilst the **East Hill Railway**, the steepest in England, takes passengers to the cliff top and the beginning of **Hastings Country Park.** The town's pier had to be repaired after World War II, when, like many others, it was deliberately holed to prevent it being used as an enemy landing stage.

Herstmonceux

The village is famous as being the home of **Herstmonceux Castle,** which was built on the site of an early Norman manor house in 1440 by Sir Roger Fiennes. It was one of the first large scale buildings in the country to be built of brick and it was also one of the first castles to combine the need for security with the comforts of the residents. The

Herstmonceux Castle

500 acres of grounds around the castle are open for most the summer. In 1948, the Royal Observatory moved here from Greenwich, and although it has since moved on again, the castle now houses the **Herstmonceux Science Centre**, where, among the domes and telescopes that the astronomers used between the 1950s and the 1980s, visitors can experience the excitement of viewing the heavens.

Horsham

Horsham's architectural gem is **The Causeway**, a quiet tree-lined street of old buildings that runs from the Georgian fronted town hall to the 12th century Church of St Mary, where can be found a simple tablet commemorating the life of Percy Bysshe Shelley, a celebrated local inhabitant. Here, too, can be found the gabled 16th century **Causeway House** - a rambling building that is now home to the **Horsham Museum**, a purpose for which its layout is ideal. Two miles southwest of Horsham lies the famous **Christ's Hospital School**, a Bluecoat school that was founded in London in 1552 by Edward VI.

Hove

Nestling at the foot of the downs and joined to Brighton, Hove is a genteel resort that is famous for its Regency squares and broad tree lined avenues. A former fishing village, Hove developed rapidly in the early 19th century when the seafront was built with its distinctive terraces. The **Hove Museum and Art Gallery**, outside which stands the splendid wooden pavilion, **Jaipur Gateway**, an elegantly carved structure that was transported to England from Rajashtan in 1886, contains a whole host of exhibits on the history of the town. For history of a different kind, the **British Engineerium**, housed in a restored 19th century pumping station, has all manner of engines - from steam powered to electric.

Also in Hove, and rather out of place with the grand Regency squares and avenues, is **West Blatchington Windmill**. Built in the 1820s and still with all its original machinery working on all five floors, the mill has been restored and continues to grind flour.

Lewes

The county town of East Sussex, Lewes is a historic settlement that occupies a strategically important point where the

Lewes Castle

River Ouse is crossed by an ancient east to west land route. William de Warenne, friend of William the Conqueror, began the construction of **Lewes Castle** and founded the great **Priory of St Pancras**. Today, a substantial part of the castle remains, including a section of the keep and two towers dating from the 13th century.

Lower Beeding

South of the village lies the beautiful **Leonardslee Gardens**, in a natural valley created by a tributary of the River Adur. Laid out by Sir Edmund Loder from 1889, the gardens are still maintained by the family and are world famous for the spring displays of azaleas, magnolias and rhododendrons around the seven landscaped lakes.

Midhurst

The grand estate here is **Cowdray** and the splendid Tudor courtyard mansion was in its day a rival to Hampton Court. Even though the house is now in ruins, it is still a splendid monument to courtly Tudor architecture. However, most visitors come to **Cowdray Park** to watch the polo matches that take place every weekend and sometimes during the week from April until July.

Newhaven

Two of the earliest visitors to use the passenger steamer service from Newhaven to Dieppe were the fleeing King and Queen of France, Louis Philippe and Marie Amelie who stayed at the Bridge Inn in 1848 after their sea journey before continuing to London by train where they were met by Queen Victoria's coach and taken to Buckingham Palace. In order to maintain their anonymity, the couple registered themselves at the inn under the rather original names of Mr and Mrs Smith. Also in the 19th century, during one of the periodic French invasion scares, **Newhaven Fort** was built. Today, it is a **Museum** where visitors can explore the underground tunnels and galleries and view the permanent Home Front exhibition.

Ninfield

To the north of the village lies Ashburnham Place, a redbrick house set in a landscaped park. **Ashburnham Park** has survived much as it was conceived by Capability Brown in the 18th century, though a large number of trees were lost in the hurricane of 1987.

North Lancing

This attractive downland village is dominated by **Lancing College**. Set high up on a beautiful site overlooking the River Adur, the college was founded in 1848 by Nathaniel Woodward, whose aim was to establish a group of classless schools. Of the college buildings, the splendid 19th century Gothic chapel is the most striking.

Northiam

Of the several notable buildings in the

Great Dixter House and Gardens

village, **Brickwall House** is an imposing 17th century gentleman's residence set in gardens that include some splendid topiary, an arboretum and a chess garden. Now a private school, the house and grounds are open by appointment only.

Just three miles northwest of Northiam lies **Great Dixter House and Gardens**, one of the finest examples of a late medieval hall house, surrounded by a very special garden. Northiam is on the **Kent and East Sussex Railway**, which was restored in 1990 and has steam trains running on a track between Tenterden in Kent and Bodiam during the summer months.

Petworth

What brings most visitors to Petworth is the grand estate of **Petworth House**, built towards the end of the 17th century and looking more like a French château than an English country house. The house is home to one of the finest art collections outside London. Just south of

the estate is the **Coultershaw Water Wheel and Beam Pump**, one of the earliest pumped water systems, installed in 1790 to pipe water two miles to Petworth House.

Pevensey

On the coast, in the shelter of Pevensey Bay, Pevensey was the landing place for invading Roman legions and it was here they built a fortification to protect their anchorage. **Pevensey Castle** seemed well able to withstand attack, and indeed, following the Battle of Lewes, Simon de Montfort laid siege here without success. However, the structure gradually fell into disrepair although it was brought back into service, briefly, during the advance of the Spanish Armada and again during World War II.

Pulborough

The centre of Pulborough, on the old Roman route, is now a conservation area with several fine Georgian cottages clustered around the parish church, which occupies a commanding hilltop position. Just southeast of the village lies the **RSPB Pulborough Brooks Nature Reserve** where there is a nature trail through tree-lined lanes, leading to views overlooking the restored wet meadows of the Arun Valley.

Rye

Rye Harbour Nature Reserve, on the mouth of the River Rother, is a large area of sea, saltmarsh, sand and shingle which supports a wide range of both plant, animal and bird life. Rye's prominent hill top position was a factor in its being a strategically important town from early times. A substantial

Mermaid Street

perimeter wall was built to defend the northern approaches and one of its four gateways, the **Landgate**, still survives today. This imposing structure is all that remains of the fortifications erected by Edward III in the 1340s.

One of Rye's oldest surviving buildings is **Ypres Tower**, which forms part of the **Rye Castle Museum**. Combining the traditional craft of model making with the latest electronic techniques, the **Rye Heritage Centre** presents a model of the town, complete with light and sound, that transports visitors back through the ages.

Sedlescombe

This former flourishing iron founding settlement is a now a pleasant and pretty village, stretched out along a long sloping green, where the parish pump still stands under a stone building of 1900. To the southeast of the village is the internationally renowned **Pestalozzi Children's Village**. Founded in 1959 to house children from Europe who had been displaced during World War II, the centre follows the theories of the Swiss educational reformer, Johann Heinrich Pestalozzi.

Selmeston

Selmeston is best known as the home of Vanessa Bell, the artist. Vanessa moved here to **Charleston Farmhouse** in 1916, with her art critic husband, Clive, and her lover, fellow artist Duncan Grant. Over the next 50 years, the intellectual and artist group that became known as the Bloomsbury set frequented the house. During the 1930s, the interior of the house was completely transformed as the group used their artistic skills to cover almost every wall, floor, ceiling and even the furniture with their own murals, fabrics, carpets and wallpapers.

Selsey

Among the most impressive buildings here is **Selsey Windmill**, a redbrick tower mill dating from 1820. With so many of the townsfolk dependant upon the sea for their living, a Lifeboat Station was established here in 1860. The present building was erected 100

Sussex

years later and contains an interesting little museum.

For many years the town's **East Beach** was a well-known site for smuggling, which, was a full time

Sheffield Park

occupation for many local inhabitants in the 18th century. In fact, whilst the French were in the throes of their revolution the villagers of Selsey were busy smuggling ashore over 12,000 gallons of spirits. Geographically, **Selsey Bill**, the extreme southwest of Sussex, is an island, with the English Channel on two sides, Pagham Harbour to the northeast and a brook running from the harbour to Bracklesham Bay which cuts the land off from the remainder of the Manhood Peninsular.

Sheffield Green

The village takes its name from the manor house, a Tudor building that was remodelled in the 1770s by James Wyatt for John Baker Holroyd, MP, the 1st Earl of Sheffield. At the same time as creating his mansion, **Sheffield Park**, the earl had Capability Brown and Humphrey Repton landscape the gardens. During his time here, the earl's great friend, Edward Gibbon, came to stay during the last months of his life, and it was while here that he wrote much of his epic *Decline and Fall of the Roman Empire* in the library. A later

inhabitant, the 3rd Earl, was a keen cricketer and was the first to organise the test tours between England and Australia. Though the house is in private hands, the splendid gardens belong to the National Trust and are open to the public. The village is also the terminus of the **Bluebell Railway** and the cricketing earl would surely have been pleased with the railway's success today as he was on the board of the Lewes and East Grinstead Railway that originally built the line.

Singleton

Lying in the folds of the South Downs, in the valley of the River Lavant, Singleton, is the home of the famous **Weald and Downland Open Air Museum**, which has over 40 reconstructed historic rural buildings from all over southeast England.

South Harting

One of the most attractive villages of the South Downs, South Harting has ancient thatched cottages and elegant redbrick Georgian houses. Outside the church stand the ancient village stocks, along with a whipping post, and inside, there are several monuments including one commemorating the life of Sir Harry Fetherstonhaugh of **Uppark**. Built in the 1680s, the house is superbly situated on the crest of a hill (this was not the opinion of the Duke of Wellington, who turned down the offer of the house on the grounds that the steep drive to the mansion would require replacing his exhausted horses too many times. The young HG Wells spent a great deal of time here as his mother worked at the house, and as well as exploring the grounds and gardens laid out by Humphry Repton, Wells could enjoy a self-taught education from Uppark's vast stock of books.

Tangmere

The village is still very much associated with the nearby former Battle of Britain base, RAF Tangmere and, although the runways have now been turned back into farmland or housing estates, the heroic deeds of the pilots are remembered at the local pub, The Bader Arms (named after pilot Douglas Bader) and the **Tangmere Military Aviation Museum**. The museum, based at the airfield, tells the story, through replica aircraft, photographs, pictures, models and memorabilia, of military flying from the earliest days during World War I to the present time.

West Dean

Just to the south of this pretty community of flint cottages, the land rises towards the ancient hilltop site known as **The Trundle**. The site was fortified during the Iron Age, when massive circular earth ramparts and a dry ditch were constructed. Amidst the rolling South Downs, **West Dean Gardens** reproduce a classic 19th century landscape and includes a highly acclaimed restoration of the walled kitchen garden, the 16 original glasshouses and frames dating from the 1890s, the 35 acres of ornamental grounds, the 40 acres St Roche's arboretum and the extensive landscaped park.

Wilmington

This delightful village, with its mix of building styles, shelters the historic remains of **Wilmington Priory**. Founded in the 11th century as an outpost of the Benedictine Abbey of Grestain in Normandy, the priory was well into decline by the time of the Dissolution. Many of the buildings were incorporated into a farmhouse, but other parts remain on their own including the prior's chapel, which is now the parish church of St Mary and St Peter.

Cut into the chalk of Windover Hill is Wilmington's famous **Long Man**, which took its present form in 1874. At over 235 feet, it is the largest such representation of a man in Europe. The giant, standing with a 250 foot long shaft in each hand, is remarkable as the design takes account of the slope of the hill and appears perfectly proportioned even when viewed from below.

THE ALMA

FRAMFIELD ROAD, UCKFIELD, EAST SUSSEX
TEL: 01825 762232

Directions: From junction 6 of the M25 follow the A22 due south. Continue through East Grinstead and 12 miles further on you will find Uckfield signposted just a short distance to the left.

The Alma is an elegant family-run pub located on the outskirts of Uckfield and within easy reach of the A22. Dating from the 1850s it is a splendid, stone-built structure that has been enlarged in recent years with an extension that is completely in keeping with the original

building. The immaculate frontage leads to an equally impressive interior that is decorated in a very homely fashion. Here you find new carpets, elegant tables and chairs and a bright and airy feel that is clearly kept neat and clean. The

landlady, Joy Hughes, puts a great of effort into keeping everything looking so good, and all in all this pub is a pleasant surprise.

There is food available lunchtimes, Monday to Saturday, and in the evening, Monday to Friday. The menu offers a superb selection of simple dishes, ranging from freshly cut sandwiches to mouth-watering meals, and everything is prepared to order and attractively presented. The bar is also well stocked with Harveys real ales together with other popular lagers, beers and ciders. Joy runs The Alma with the help of her son Robert and together they have created a friendly, welcoming environment that is much loved by the local community.

- 🕐 Mon-Sat 11.00-14.30, 18.00-23.00; Sun 12.00-14.00, 19.00-22.30
- 🍴 Superb range of simple dishes
- £ Visa, Mastercard, Delta, Switch, Amex, Diners
- Ⓟ Patio, car park
- ❓ Sheffield Park Garden 3 miles, Plumpton Racecourse 9 miles, Tanyard House 11 miles, Bowles Outdoor Pursuits Centre 11 miles, Glyndebourne 10 miles, Lewes Castle 9 miles

BAX CASTLE

TWO MILE ASH ROAD, SOUTHWATER, HORSHAM,
WEST SUSSEX RH13 0LA   TEL: 01403 730369

> **Directions:** From junction 9 of the M25 follow the A24 to Dorking and on to
> Horsham. Turn left onto the B2237 toward the town centre and after about a mile
> turn left again. This road will turn back on itself and take you under the A24 into
> Two Mile Ash.

The Bax Castle is a delightfully unspoilt 15th century freehouse, tucked away in the tiny village of Two Mile Ash, not far from the busy town of Horsham. A friendly pub, it has been run by Mike and Molly Porteous for the past 18 months and they have firmly established it as a favourite among the local community. The Bax Castle wins favour on three counts: good quality cheap food, and plenty of it, a decent selection of cask

ales and the early evening sun which falls on the front garden. Set well back from the road, this is a delightfully quiet spot in which to enjoy a drink on a warm day.

Inside you will find a comfortable bar area which is separate from the dining room, and there is also a non-smoking area. The well stocked bar offers a superb wine list, in addition to the beer and lager, with some well priced bottles from all over the world. A delicious menu of traditional English dishes is served each lunchtime and evening, seven days a week, with the lamb proving to be a highly popular choice.

- Mon-Sat 11.30-15.00, 18.00-23.00; Sun 12.00-15.00, 19.00-22.30 (open all day at weekends in summer)
- Large dining area
- Visa, Mastercard, Delta, Switch
- Children's play area, beer garden, car park
- Leith Hill Tower 10 miles, Gatwick Airport 12 miles, Leonardslee Gardens 7 miles, Winkworth Arboretum 14 miles, Guildford 20 miles

THE BEACH TAVERN

SEA ROAD, PEVENSEY BAY, EAST SUSSEX BN24 6EH
TEL: 01323 761372

Directions: Pevensey Bay lies 5 miles to the northeast of Eastbourne. It can be reached by taking the A22 south from junction 6 of the M25 towards the coast. Four miles from Eastbourne, Pevensey will be signposted to the left along the A27.

The appropriately named **Beach Tavern** lies just a few yards from the sea front, in this little known village lying between Eastbourne and Bexhill. The pub has recently been taken over by Tony and Karen O'Grady who come with many years experience in the pub trade, and they have spent their first few months getting the place just how they like it. Popular with the locals, it is in the summer months that it comes into its own, proving popular with tourists of

all ages, particularly with families.

The interior is mainly open plan, with the décor and furnishings being of a traditional style, in keeping with the 18th century building. There are copper-topped tables, chairs and stools to be found throughout the public bar, the lounge and in the dining area, with the atmosphere being comfortable and relaxed. Here you can enjoy some traditional English cuisine with the wide ranging menu offering snacks, pasta, curries, steaks and plenty of seafood. All dishes are fresh and tasty and offer great value for money. Food is served each lunchtime and evening in the summer season, but at lunchtime only in the winter months. Ring for details.

🕐 Mon-Sat 11.00-23.00; Sun 12.00-22.30

🍴 Traditional English cuisine (lunches only out of season)

🅿 Patio, car park

🎵 Quiz night Wednesday, pool table

@ tonyog1962@aol.com

❓ Eastbourne 5 miles, Hastings 12 miles, Herstmonceux Castle Gardens 5 miles, Beachy Head 8 miles, Michelham Priory 8 miles, Newhaven Ferry Terminal 17 miles

THE BELL INN

CHURCH LANE, IDEN, NR. RYE, EAST SUSSEX TN31 7PU
TEL: 01797 280242

Directions: Take junction 10 of the M20 and follow the by-pass around Ashford and then pick up the A2070, and then the A259, to Rye. Just as you enter the town take the A268, turning right after a mile onto the A2082 which will lead you to Iden.

Not far from the historic town of Rye lies the typical Sussex village that is Iden. Like most small villages, **The Bell Inn**, the local pub, dominates the main street. The pub has origins in the 12th century when there was an ale house on the site, run by monks and although the present structure is much later, it is clearly carrying on in a similar tradition. The newest owners are Steve and Sue Trendle, and they have some great plans for the place: a programme of refurbishment is planned, with the intention being to retain all the interesting, original features of the building, and adding a fresh new décor.

- Mon-Sat 11.00-23.00; Sun 12.00-22.30
- Excellent cuisine offering great value
- Visa, Mastercard, Delta, Switch
- Two rooms with four-poster beds
- Beer garden, car park
- Quiz night Mondays
- Rye 2 miles, Kent & East Sussex Railway 8 miles, Great Dixter House and Gardens 8 miles, Bodiam Castle 12 miles, Hastings 15 miles, Smallhythe Place 6 miles

They will continue as a free house with the bar stocking a selection of real ales together with other popular beers and lagers. Some tasty food can be enjoyed here too, with the excellent menu of home-cooked dishes ranging from snacks to local beef and fresh seafood. Meals can be taken either in the bar or the separate 32-cover restaurant which is located to the rear. Food is available every lunchtime and Tuesday to Saturday evenings. In a converted cottage which lies alongside the pub, there is bed and breakfast accommodation available. The two guest rooms are each furnished with a four-poster bed and are provided with en-suite facilities, colour TV and complimentary hot drinks tray. Reasonable rates – ring for details.

Sussex

THE BREWERS ARMS

GARDNER STREET, HERSTMONCEUX, EAST SUSSEX BN27 4LB
TEL: 01323 832226

Directions: From junction 10 of the M23 take the A264 towards East Grinstead, picking up the A22 after about 5 miles signposted for Eastbourne. As you approach Hailsham take the A271 to the left where you will find Herstmonceux after about 5 miles

The Brewers Arms is a charming, village pub with origins in the 16th century, and has recently been refurbished inside and out to an exceedingly high standard by the present owners, Barry and Barbara Dimmack. The couple are past winners of the Greene King National pub hosts of the year, and together with their friendly staff look after every customer, both old and new, very well indeed.

In addition to the two lovely beamed bars there is also a restaurant with a non-smoking area and outside a most attractive garden. The pub boasts some very attractive objects d'art and a magnificent collection of antique wall and grandfather clocks. The menu is

🕐 Mon-Sat 11.00-14.30, 18.00-23.00;
Sun 12.00-15.00, 19.00-22.30

🍴 Tasty home-made food

💷 Visa, Mastercard, Delta, Switch

🅿 Beer garden and patio, car park

❓ Herstmonceux Castle Gardens 2 miles, Wartling Nature Reserve 2 miles, Eastbourne 13 miles, Bateman's House 10 miles, Michelham Priory 5 miles

excellent, offering a wide range of delicious dishes, including curries, pasta and home-cooked pies, with a good fish selection each day too. Food is served at lunchtimes and in the evening Monday through to Sunday (except Tuesday) with everything being freshly prepared to order and offering great value for money. The quality of the food has achieved such a reputation that a number of regular customers travel from all over the southeast just to eat here. Regrettably children under 14 are not permitted in the pub, although dogs with well-behaved owners are most welcome. This is a truly traditional village pub - warm, comfortable and friendly - with great beers and excellent food. Highly recommended.

CATTS INN

HIGH STREET, ROTHERFIELD, EAST SUSSEX TN6 3LH
TEL: 01892 852546

Directions: From Royal Tunbridge Wells follow the A267 due south. After 5 miles turn right onto the B2100. After about two miles you will come to Rotherfield.

In the centre of Rotherfield, looking very much like a private home, is **Catts Inn**. Built in the 16th century it was originally an alehouse, later becoming an inn, named after the local Catt family who were once Lords of the Manor. This traditional village hostelry is a freehouse, ably owned and

managed by Fred and Monica Jones who have been landlords here since 1990, having previously masterminded the Royal British Legion at Horsted Keynes. They welcome all customers with the assistance of the newest family member, young Buster, who is a friendly terrier.

Unusually it is Fred who masterminds the kitchen offering a daily selection of

🕐 Mon-Fri 11.30-15.00, 18.30-23.00; Sat 11.00-23.00; Sun 11.00-22.30

🍴 Good food at reasonable prices

Ⓟ Patio garden

🎵 Darts, crib, regular quiz nights

❓ Royal Tunbridge Wells 7 miles, Sheffield Park Garden 12 miles, Bateman's 9 miles, Bayham Abbey 11 miles, Tanyard House 12 miles.

meals and snacks. All the dishes are cooked to order, even the chips are homemade, with everything also being sensibly priced. Food is available at lunchtimes and in the evening, seven days a week. The food is complemented by a well-stocked bar offering a choice of two real ales and a selection of bottled beers and ciders. Popular with locals, visitors are made more than welcome here but be warned this is a rather lively establishment. Most nights there is entertainment of some sort - crib tournaments, darts, quizzes - and at the weekends they'll all be playing football! Much of the activity is put to a good cause, raising funds for a local surgery, so you may well be asked to donate to the latest appeal.

Sussex

CHARCOAL BURNER

WEALD DRIVE, FURNACE GREEN, CRAWLEY, WEST SUSSEX RH10 6NY
TEL: 01293 653981

Directions: Crawley can be found just off junction 10 of the M23. Furnace Green lies to the southeast of the town. Follow signs to Hawth Theatre.

The Charcoal Burner may at first glance appear to be tucked away on the back streets of Crawley, however it lies next to the 38 acre wooded site of the Hawth Theatre, one of the most exciting arts venues in the southeast. The pub dates back to the 1960s and is typical of the style of the era. The outside has recently been repainted and so looks bright and cheerful, with a bright red sign and matching fence. Inside, the spacious interior is split into two distinctive areas – the public bar and the lounge. Like the outside it has recently been upgraded and is spotlessly clean and comfortably furnished throughout. The

regular clientele, drawn from the surrounding area, is a real mixture of ages, with families, OAPs and sporty types all coming to enjoy the relaxed surroundings.

The bar stocks a range of beers and lagers, all kept in tip top condition, together with bottled beers and the alcopops that are so popular these days. If you like to enjoy some tasty food with your drinks, there is a good menu of homemade dishes available from midday until 9pm, seven days a week. There is plenty to choose from, though the grills feature prominently and appear to be a popular selection. The meals are reasonably priced too. The chef is owner Janice Pierce, and she has plenty of experience in the catering trade, which shows.

- 🕐 Mon-Sat 11.00-23.00; Sun 12.00-22.30
- 🍴 Food available all day until 9pm
- £ Visa, Mastercard, Delta, Switch
- Ⓟ Patio area
- ♪ Quiz on Tuesdays, occasional karaoke, pool table
- @ janblackcat@aol.com
- ❓ Gatwick Airport 3 miles, Leonardslee Gardens 8 miles, Leith Hill Tower 11 miles, Nutfield Priory 10 miles, Tanyard House 10 miles, Polesden Lacey 14 miles

FORESTERS ARMS

KIRDFORD, NR. BILLINGSHURST, WEST SUSSEX RH14 0ND
TEL: 01403 820205

Directions: From junction 9 of the M25, take the A24 south through Dorking to Beare Green. At the roundabout turn right onto the A29 to Billingshurst and then turn right onto the A272. Kirdford will be signposted to the left after about 4 miles.

The Foresters Arms is a 17th century former coaching inn, well hidden from passers-by in the tiny rural village of Kirdford, overlooking the village green. The original structure has been added to many times over the years, resulting in the

substantial establishment that you see here today and there are many charming features that have been retained inside and out giving it a great deal of character. The cosy interior retains the open log fires and stone floors and a rustic relaxed ambience can be enjoyed throughout.

Most of the regular customers come here for the delicious home-cooked food that is on offer. The menu presents a selection of traditional English snacks and hot dishes, all prepared to order using the freshest ingredients, complemented by a daily specials board. Food is available at lunchtimes, seven days a week, and Tuesday to Saturday evenings until 9.00pm. In warmer weather meals and drinks can be taken outside in the beer garden, where you can also try your hand at boules. Occasionally there is the option of a lively night out with jazz or folk music.

- Mon-Sat 11.00-15.00, 18.00-23.00; Sun 12.00-22.30
- Delicious, home-cooked, English dishes
- Visa, Mastercard, Delta, Switch
- Boules pitch, beer garden, car park
- Occasional jazz and folk music
- Petworth House 5 miles, Black Down Nature Trail 8 miles, Arundel Castle 14 miles, Bignor Roman Villa 10 miles, Winkworth Arboretum 11 miles, Guildford 21 miles

THE LAMB INN

WARTLING ROAD, WARTLING, HAILSHAM, EAST SUSSEX BN27 1RY
TEL: 01323 832116

Directions: From junction 6 of the M25 follow the A22 south. As you approach Hailsham take the A271 to the left and after 5 miles Wartling will be signposted to the right.

In the village of Wartling, not far from the A259 south coast road, you will find a welcome stopping-off point at the **Lamb Inn.** Standing beside the village church, not far from Herstmonceux castle, this is a delightful 16th-century former coaching inn with bundles of character. The building has probably changed little over the centuries with the elevated, white-washed frontage retaining the old, small paned windows and original doors.

Inside there are no less than three log fires, low ceilings, oak beams and tiled floors throughout, with the space made up of numerous nooks and crannies in which to tuck yourself away. Here, in a warm friendly atmosphere the delicious aroma of freshly cooked food mingles with the smell of the log fires and you can soak up the olde worlde ambience while sampling a wide range of beers and lagers. The superb menu offers what is described as modern English cuisine, with an extensive variety of dishes at very reasonable prices. You can usually find steak, game, poultry and up to four different types of fresh fish available on any single day, with Alison specialising in quality local produce. Whether you want a refreshing drink or a tasty meal out, the Lamb Inn, run by husband and wife team, Robert and Alison Farncombe, is an ideal place to try.

🕐 Tue-Sat 11.00-15.00, 18.30-23.00; Sun 12.00-15.00. Summer hours may vary.

🍴 Modern English cuisine

£ Visa, Mastercard, Delta, Switch, Amex

P Beer garden, car park

? Wartling Nature Reserve 1 mile, Herstmonceux Castle Gardens 1 mile, Eastbourne 9 miles, Hastings 12 miles, Bateman's House 12 miles, Michelham Priory 10 miles

MALT SHOVEL

22 SPRINGFIELD ROAD, HORSHAM, SUSSEX RH12 2PG
TEL: 01403 254543

> **Directions:** Leave the M25 at junction 9 and follow the A24 south where after about 18 miles the town of Horsham will be signposted to the left.

Conveniently located in the heart of the thriving town of Horsham lies the imposing **Malt Shovel** public house. Rebuilt in the 1930s, the original inn sat on what is now a traffic island and was once a small brewery. It was called the Michele Brewery, and over time the name was gradually amended to the present title.

As you might expect, when you learn of its heritage, this is a real ale pub where the well-stocked bar can offer no less than nine varieties at any one time. Not only has this led to the pub being featured in CAMRA's Good Beer Guide since 1998, but there is also an annual Beer Festival held in the first week of September each year. It has also been known for real cider to be available here too.

If you are in need of a bite to eat with your pint, then a delicious selection of food is served from midday until 5pm daily (until 8pm on Monday, Tuesday, Thursday and Friday). The meals are all home-made using only the freshest ingredients, served in hearty portions at tiny prices. There is a board of daily specials and there are regular curry nights. The impressive red brick frontage leads to a characterful interior of oak floors and wooden panelling and the friendly landlord is Steve Williams whose other passion is rugby.

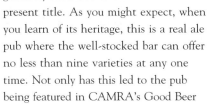

- Mon-Sat 11.00-23.00; Sun 12.00-22.30
- Fresh, tasty home-made food
- Visa, Mastercard, Delta, Switch
- Patio, car park
- Quiz on Sundays
- steve@maltshovel.com
- Gatwick Airport 9 miles, Leonardslee Gardens 6 miles, Petworth House 16 miles, St, Leonards Forest Trails 4 miles, Leith Hill Tower 10 miles, Guildford 19 miles

THE OLDE BELL INN

HIGH STREET, RYE, EAST SUSSEX TN31 7EN
TEL: 01797 223323 FAX: 01797 229131

Directions: From junction 9 of the M20, head into Ashford and take the A2070 due south, turning onto the A259 at Brenzett following signs for Rye.

The historic port of Rye is full of interesting old buildings, and **The Olde Bell Inn** on the High Street is no exception. Dating back to the early 15th century, the exterior appearance has hardly changed over the centuries while inside you will find a cosy and compact bar with the original beams crossing the ceiling above your head. Like many inns of the time, there are stories of smugglers using the inn for passing on their contraband, and it is easy to believe that there were indeed secret doorways and hidden passages at one time.

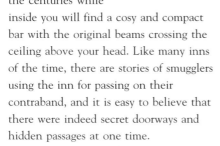

Mon-Sat 11.00-23.00; Sun 12.00-22.30

Fresh, tasty food served 12-4pm

Patio beer garden

Lamb House, Dungeness Nature Reserve 12 miles, Hastings 12 miles, Kent & East Sussex Railway 11 miles, Bodiam Castle 11 miles, Great Dixter House and Gardens 9 miles

Conveniently located close to the centre of town, this makes a popular eating and drinking spot for both locals and tourists. The menu offers a wide range of home-made dishes, mainly traditional English cuisine, and all superbly cooked and beautifully presented. Food is available from midday until 4pm each day, and during July and August is served up until 7pm. In summer months it is also possible to enjoy your meal outside on the patio, where you can watch the world go by. A charming town centre inn that is simply oozing historic character, where you can be assured of a friendly welcome, a refreshing pint, and a tasty meal. Well worth a try.

THE PARK TAVERN

11 PRIORY ROAD, CHICHESTER, WEST SUSSEX PO19 1NS
TEL: 01243 785057

Directions: Chichester can be readily located just off the A27 coast road, which is a continuation of the M27.

The Park Tavern lies just a short walk from the centre of Chichester, which has much to offer the visitor with interesting old buildings and a most attractive cathedral. This 17th-century hostelry enjoys a prime corner site and boasts a recently upgraded, handsome frontage. Inside there is a traditional feel to both bar areas, with the public bar being cosy and compact while the lounge area is much more spacious. The décor reflects the owner's love of Dublin and all things Irish but be assured, this is not a run of the mill Irish-themed pub. Indeed you couldn't get further from it, because Richard

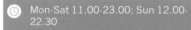

- Mon-Sat 11.00-23.00; Sun 12.00-22.30
- Authentic Thai food
- Visa, Mastercard, Delta, Switch
- Car park
- Occasional theme nights
- Chichester Festival Theatre, Chichester Cathedral, Goodwood House 2 miles, Kingley Vale National Nature Reserve 5 miles, Goodwood Racecourse 4 miles, Bognor Regis 6 miles, Fishbourne Roman Villa 2 miles

Thompson runs the place with his Thai partner, Thippawan Charoenlip.

The culinary pairing results in an outstanding menu of authentic Thai cuisine, with overtones of traditional English pub fayre for those that prefer. The mouth-watering menu has plenty to choose from, with fresh local seafood used extensively. To enjoy with your meal the bar presents an extensive wine list together with some fine real ales. Food is available each lunchtime and from 6pm until late each evening. If you don't like the idea of sacrificing one of the best of English culinary traditions, then you can enjoy a roast lunch here each Sunday. The Park Tavern is popular with a wide variety of locals, ranging from office workers to students, and is well worth seeking out if you are simply visiting the area.

Sussex

THE PLOUGH

IFIELD STREET, CRAWLEY, WEST SUSSEX RH11 0NN
TEL/FAX: 01292 524292

> **Directions:** Leaving the M23 at junction 10, follow the A2011 dual carriageway around Crawley. Continue over the roundabout at the junction with the A23 and turn right towards Ifield at the next roundabout.

Ifield was originally a village in its own right before it was absorbed into the edge of the new town of Crawley, however it has since been designated as a Conservation Area because it retains its character as a small scattered rural settlement. **The Plough Inn** can be found in the heart of the conservation area and lies alongside the 13th century church. In fact, there has been a pub here since around the same time, though the present structure was built in the 1920s alongside the original building.

Venturing inside the pub you will find everything to be of a very high quality and immaculately maintained, combined

- ⏰ Mon-Thur 11.00-15.00, 18.00-23.00, Fri-Sat 11.00-16.00, 18.00-23.00, Sun 19.00-22.30 (Sat-Sun longer opening hours in summer)
- 🍴 Simple menu of home-cooked dishes
- £ Visa, Mastercard, Delta, Switch
- 🅿 Patio, car park
- @ davejack@witzend30.fsnet.co.uk
- ❓ Tilgate Park 3 miles, Ifield Water Mill 1 Mile, Gatwick Airport 4 miles, Leith Hill Tower 10 miles, Leonardslee Gardens 10 miles, Nutfield Priory 10 miles, Tanyard House 11 miles, Red and Green Circular walks

with an atmosphere that is warm and welcoming. The owners, Dave and Jacqueline Harding, are responsible for the high standards and in their year here have won over most of the local community. They come here to enjoy the fine selection of quality real ales and the excellent wine list, and the food is equally good, all home-cooked using only the best ingredients. The menus are simple but offer an excellent choice of popular dishes, such as pasta, steaks, pies and chicken, and a good range of light snacks. Food is served Monday to Saturday at lunchtime and in the evening.

PRINCE OF WALES

HAILSHAM ROAD, HEATHFIELD, EAST SUSSEX TN21 8DR
TEL: 01435 862919 FAX: 01435 868183

Directions: From junction 10 of the M23, follow the A264 all the way to Royal Tunbridge Wells. Then take the A267 due south and after 15 miles you will reach Heathfield.

The Prince of Wales is a large and impressive inn, occupying a prominent site on a busy crossroads and something of a local landmark.

An historic hostelry dating back a few hundred years, it has been recently taken

over by Martin Mackenzie who has previously run pubs in Brighton. He has plans to completely refurbish the whole place, inside and out, which will undoubtedly take him some time, but will result in a fresh, modern feel throughout.

- Mon-Sat 11.00-23.00; Sun 12.00-22.30
- Inventive cuisine with ever-changing menus
- Visa, Mastercard, Delta, Switch
- Front patio area, car park
- Bentley Wildfowl Centre 8 miles, Michelham Priory 8 miles, Batemans House 7 miles, Royal Tunbridge Wells 15 miles, Sheffield Park Garden 11 miles, Lewes Castle 14 miles

The overall layout will not be changing, and inside you will continue to find a lounge and a public bar together with a delightful conservatory restaurant. It is clear that the restaurant is the focus of attention with most of the mixed clientele coming here to enjoy the fine food.

The dining area is large, with 72 covers, and well laid out and you can be fairly sure of finding a table at most of the sessions. The menus feature a wide range of inventive dishes and are regularly updated to make the most of seasonally available produce.

Food is served lunchtimes and until 9pm in the evening, Monday to Saturday. On Sundays food is served midday until 3pm.

THE RAM INN

FIRLE, NR. LEWES, EAST SUSSEX BN8 6NS
TEL: 01273 858222

Directions: From the end of the M23, follow the A23 towards Brighton. When you reach the A27 turn left and follow it to Lewes, and then on towards Eastbourne. About 4 miles beyond Lewes, past the turning for the A26, Firle is signposted on the left.

Sitting on a quiet tree lined lane in the tranquil backwater of Firle, **The Ram Inn** is an attractive, unspoilt country pub that remains relatively unchanged since it was built in the 16th century. There is a main bar, a quiet non-smoking snug area and a large family room provided with games, toys and high chairs. In the summer, food and drink can be enjoyed in the delightful sheltered gardens, where there is a children's play area and a separate hidden garden, ideal for quiet dining. In winter months the log fires in the bar and snug create a warm and cosy atmosphere.

The Ram serves traditional pub food every day, from midday until 9pm, with a scrumptious Sussex cream tea available from 3pm until 5.30pm. As well as the delicious, wide-ranging menu, there is also a special children's menu and tins of babyfood available, with all the facilities you may need for heating up bottles and food. The bar stocks three real ales, including Harveys, and a traditional hand-pulled cider. There is a large range of soft drink and a selection of children's drinks too.

This is a friendly pub, family run by Nik and Keith Wooller who are busy, working parents with four young children of their own. They describe The Ram as a traditional Sussex pub run by parents, for parents.

- Mon-Sat 11.30-23.00; Sun 12.00-22.30
- Traditional pub food served all day
- Visa, Mastercard, Delta, Switch
- Children's play area, beer garden, parking, excellent baby facilities
- Live folk music monthly, pub quiz monthly
- e-mail: nikwooler@raminnfirle.net website: www.raminnfirle.net
- Firle Place, Charleston Farmhouse 2 miles, Glyndebourne 3 miles, Lewes Castle 5 miles, Michelham Priory 8 miles, Brighton 12 miles, Seven Sisters Country Park 10 miles

ROSE AND CROWN

HAM LANE, BURWASH, EAST SUSSEX TN19 7ER
TEL/FAX: 01435 882600

Directions: From the A21 at Hurst Green take the A265 heading west. Burwash is about 4 miles. Ham Lane is part way along the High Street on the right hand side.

The Rose and Crown is a traditional Sussex village inn dating back to the 15th century. Presenting a pretty picture with its low doorways, small paned windows and prominent brick chimneys, inside you will find low, beamed ceilings with a bar and separate restaurant, attractively decorated with many interesting pictures on the walls. In winter months you can snuggle up around the blazing log fires while in summer you might choose to enjoy the country air on the spacious patio or in the sunny beer garden.

The cosy intimate restaurant, laid out with fresh linen and good quality glass and tableware, is the perfect place to enjoy the a la carte menu. Alternatively, you may simply want a tasty bar snack,

with a superb selection ranging from filled baguettes to traditional bar meals, with a more interesting blackboard 'specials' menu too. The well stocked bar, which is cask marque accredited, offers a range from the Harveys Brewery, together with other popular lagers, draught cider and Guinness. There is also a good quality wine list.

If you would like to linger in the area, and there is certainly plenty to see and do here, there are three guest bedrooms available for bed and breakfast. Each is cosy and comfortably furnished, and provided with tea and coffee making facilities, colour TV and en-suite shower room.

Both members of the British Institute of Innkeepers, the licensees, Ted and Maggie Hirst, are committed to developing the full potential of the Rose and Crown by offering a warm friendly welcome and a relaxing atmosphere.

- Mon-Sat 11.00-23.00; Sun 12.00-22.30
- Bar snacks and meals and a full a la carte menu
- Visa, Mastercard, Delta, Switch
- 1 double, 2 twin, all with en-suite shower room
- www.roseandcrownburwash.co.uk
- Patio and beer garden, car park
- Occasional live music, quiz on Wednesdays, pub games, darts

ROSE AND CROWN

CODMORE HILL, PULBOROUGH, WEST SUSSEX RH20 1BG
TEL: 01798 873692

> **Directions:** From junction 9 of the M25, take the A24 south through Dorking to Beare Green. At the roundabout turn right onto the A29 which will take you through Billingshurst and about 4 miles further on is Codmore Hill.

If you like the friendliness of a family-run pub, then the **Rose and Crown** in Codmore Hill will be right up your street. Recently taken on by Ray Grant, a former fisherman, and his wife Carol, they run the place with the assistance of their children. In their short

time here the family have already embarked on an extensive programme of refurbishment giving the place a fresher feel.

Despite the cosmetic improvements

the emphasis remains on a relaxed, comfortable environment in which to enjoy a refreshing drink and a tasty bite to eat. The spacious interior offer plenty of seating while the open log fires keep the surroundings warm and cosy in cooler weather.

With both Ray and Carol liking to cook, the menu offers a wide variety of dishes with mainly traditional English cuisine. The specialities are the home-made pies and, as a reflection of Ray's former career, fresh fish is served daily. Food is available Monday to Saturday at lunchtime and in the evening, and for Sunday lunch midday until 4pm. In the summer months, drinks can be enjoyed in the beer garden, and there is also plenty of car parking.

🕐 Mon-Thurs 11.00-15.00, 18.00-23.00; Fri-Sat 11.00-23.00; Sun 12.00-22.30

🍺 Traditional English cuisine

💷 Visa, Mastercard, Delta, Switch

🅿 Beer garden, car park

🎵 Occasional pub quiz, pool, darts

❓ Bignor Roman Villa 6 miles, Petworth House 5 miles, Goodwood Racecourse 14 miles, Chichester 16 miles, Arundel Castle 9 miles, Arundel Wildfowl Trust 9 miles, Cissbury Ring 12 miles

ROYAL OAK

HIGH STREET, BARCOMBE, NEAR LEWES, EAST SUSSEX BN8 5BA
TEL: 01273 400418

Directions: From the end of the M23 follow the A23 to Brighton and then the A27 west to Lewes. From the centre of the town turn onto the A275 for 1 mile to Offham, and then turn right following signs to Barcombe.

Tucked away in the quaint little village of Barcombe is the charming **Royal Oak** public house. Dating from the early 16th century it was originally a couple of cottages, and thankfully much of the historic character has been retained. The front is neatly presented, with hanging baskets adorning every corner, a table or two for making the most of any fine weather, with further tables in the well maintained beer garden and children's play area to the rear of the pub. Inside the traditional feel is continued, with thick carpets, wooden tables and chairs, and attentive experienced staff to help you feel right at home. It is not surprising that there is such a friendly feel to the place as, rather unusually in this business, the owners Mike and Caroline Austen have been here for over 20 years and firmly established the Royal Oak as a favourite drinking spot among the local community.

Not only do the regulars come here to enjoy a fine pint, but the food also has a far-reaching reputation. The quality of the fayre equals that of many a restaurant, but at your regular pub prices, serving in surroundings that are elegant and stylish. The style is traditional English cuisine, all freshly prepared and cooked to your requirements. To round off your meal to perfection there is a delicious selection of wicked desserts. Food available every lunchtime and most evenings (no food Sunday or Monday nights).

- 🕐 Mon-Sat 11.00-14.30, 18.00-23.00; Sun 12.00-14.30, 19.00-22.30
- 🍴 Restaurant quality food
- £ Visa, Mastercard, Delta, Switch, Amex, Diners
- Ⓟ Skittle alley, function room, beer garden, children's play area, car park
- @ em-royaloak@supanet.com
- ? Lewes Castle 3 miles, Glyndebourne 5 miles, Plumpton Racecourse 7 miles, Brighton 11 miles, Sheffield Park 8 miles, Michelham Priory 13 miles

THE ROYAL OAK

PETT ROAD, PETT, NR. HASTINGS, EAST SUSSEX TN35 4HG
TEL: 01424 812515 FAX: 01424 814733

Directions: If you are travelling clockwise on the M25 then you can readily pick up the A21 at junction 5 and follow it all the way to Hastings on the coast. When you reach the centre of the town, take the A259 to the left and Pett will be signposted to your right after about 3 miles.

The Royal Oak is a large country inn that enjoys a quiet location away from the hustle and bustle of the town of Hastings. This is a thinly populated area, but the coastline is lovely and this would make a nice trip out of Hastings or Rye for lunch or a evening meal. The large pub is under the ownership of Jasmine Wan and she runs the place with help from her mother and brothers, giving it a real friendly, family-run feel. In her 12 months here she has won back much of the local trade together with new customers from all over the area, and tourists.

The open plan interior retains much of its original charm and features, such as the huge inglenook fireplace, combined with new carpets and numerous tables and chairs. Much of the pub's popularity is due to the fine food on offer with an extensive menu of home-cooked dishes catering to all tastes. The highlights are fresh lobster, when available, and the monthly gourmet game weekends (ring for details). Food is served at lunchtime and in the evening through the week and all day Saturday and Sunday until 9pm (until 10pm on Saturday).

- Mon-Sat 11.00-23.00; Sun 12.00-22.30
- Extensive menu with daily specials
- Visa, Mastercard, Delta, Switch
- Beer garden, car park
- Rye 6 miles, Hastings 5 miles, Bodiam Castle 15 miles, Herstmonceux Castle Gardens 18 miles, Great Dixter House and Gardens 11 miles, Kent & East Sussex Railway 13 miles

THE SMUGGLER

Sussex

PETT LEVEL ROAD, PETT LEVEL, NR. HASTINGS,
EAST SUSSEX TN35 4EH
TEL/FAX: 01424 813491

Directions: From the M25 take the A21 south to Hastings on the coast. Take the A259 out of Hastings towards Rye and after a mile or so turn right onto a minor coast road passing through the village of Fairlight and onto Pett Level.

The name and location of **The Smuggler Inn** would lead some to believe that there is fascinating history of pirates and contraband to be unearthed. Unfortunately this isn't so - the building on this site was originally a beach club becoming an inn only 25 years ago. However, the relatively modern history hasn't prevented this from being a characterful establishment with a cosy interior and welcoming atmosphere; in the winter months the warm welcome is enhanced by the open fires.

The extensive rear beer garden and

patio area overlooking the sea are perhaps the most popular feature, being an enjoyable place to enjoy a drink or a meal. The pub is only a short walk from the dramatic coastline with numerous scenic footpaths. Inside you will find a comfortable interior with upholstered seating and chunky furniture, all spotlessly clean. There is a non-smoking restaurant area although food is served throughout the pub. The menu offers a good range of dishes all freshly cooked and simply served with no frills, just offering good value for money. Food is available every lunchtime and evening with a superb carvery on Saturday evenings and Sunday lunchtime. Behind the bar is an equally fine selection of traditional beers and lagers .

Mon-Sat 11.00-15.00, 18.00-23.00;
Sun 12.00-15.00, 18.00-22.30
(variable weekend opening in
summer months)

Bar and restaurant menus

Visa, Mastercard, Delta, Switch

Beer garden and patio, car park,
games room

Coastal footpaths, Hastings 4 miles,
Rye 7 miles, Great Dixter House
and Gardens 13 miles, Bodiam
Castle 13 miles, Herstmonceux
Castle Gardens 17 miles,
Smallhythe House 16 miles

Sussex

THE SUSSEX OAK

2 CHURCH STREET, WARNHAM, NR. HORSHAM,
WEST SUSSEX RH12 3QW
TEL: 01403 265028 FAX: 01403 265128

Directions: From junction 9 of the M25 follow the A24 to beyond Dorking. As you approach Horsham, Warnham is signposted to the right

Located just off the A24, **The Sussex Oak** makes a convenient stopping place for those exploring or passing through the area by car. Set well back from the road, this attractive country inn is nice and quiet and has a lovely beer garden with mature trees which is a lovely place to sit and enjoy your drink.

Dating back to the 17th century, this former coaching inn has been greatly extended and well looked after over the year, and today presents an attractive, freshly painted frontage. Inside you will find a traditionally styled interior with luxurious couches, oak tables and chairs and a thick carpet under foot, all kept extra cosy in winter months by the open fires.

With seating for up to 80 diners, it is clear that that Sussex Oak has a popular reputation for serving good, tasty food. The menu is described as a combination of modern English and traditional cuisine, and features a range of delicious dishes from around the globe. Presented on three blackboards scattered around the pub, the selection is regularly updated to make the most of seasonally available produce. Food is served at lunchtimes and in the evening, except Sunday and Monday nights.

- 🕐 Mon-Sat 11.00-23.00; Sun 12.00-22.30
- 🍴 Modern English and traditional cuisine
- £ Visa, Mastercard, Delta, Switch
- Ⓟ Beer garden, car park
- 🎵 Bar billiards, darts
- @ sussexoakwarnham@aol.com
- ❓ Leith Hill Tower 7 miles, Gatwick Airport 12 miles, Wakehurst Place Gardens 13 miles, Winkworth Arboretum 12 miles, Guildford 20 miles

WINDSOR TAVERN

165 LANGNEY ROAD, EASTBOURNE, EAST SUSSEX BN22 8AH
TEL: 01323 726206

> **Directions:** From junction 6 of the M25 take the A22 due south to Eastbourne, a distance of around 44 miles.

Not far from the centre of the ever popular resort of Eastbourne, the **Windsor Tavern** sits alongside a busy road. Formerly fishermen's cottages, the elegant, classic, white building stands out from its neighbours in the surrounding area. Dating back to the late 18th century, the building has been a public house since the late 19th century.

Leaseholders, Dave and Sue Harding are a local couple who have breathed a new lease of life into the place and established a reputation for serving quality food and a well kept range of ales which include Abbot Ale and a rotating guest ale. Add to this a decent range of beers, ciders and

- Mon-Sat 11.00-23.00; Sun 12.00-22.30
- Well presented, home cooked pub food
- Beer garden, on street parking
- Sunday night pub quiz, occasional theme nights, race nights and discos
- Beachy Head 3 miles, Seven Sisters Country Park 7 miles, Newhaven Ferry Terminal 13 miles, Charleston Farmhouse 11 miles, Michelham Priory 9 miles, Herstmonceaux Castle Gardens 10 miles

Guinness and the choice is ample. Food is honest, home-cooked English favourites, served in a straightforward style and very reasonably priced. Dishes include familiar combinations like gammon and pineapple and liver and bacon. Lighter bites and a children's menu are also available while on Sundays there is a traditional roast lunch. Food is a big thing here, and every few weeks on a Wednesday there's a special food themed evening, but be sure to book a space as they are understandably very popular. To the rear, there is a sunny beer garden where barbeques are held on summer weekends and occasionally a bouncy castle is arranged for entertaining the children.

Sussex

YE OLDE HOUSE AT HOME

77 EAST BROADWATER STREET, BROADWATER, WORTHING,
WEST SUSSEX BN14 9AD
TEL: 01903 232661 FAX: 01903 207053

Directions: From junction 9 of the M25 you can follow the A24 directly to
Worthing where Broadwater can be found on the outskirts of the town.

Ye Olde House at Home is an interesting looking pub with an attractive frontage that seems to be all windows and stonework. The location is convenient for the local shops and looks out over the

expansive green where in summer months cricket is played. The pub has been run for the past two years by a delightful young couple, Sarah and Graham Roy, and they have established this as a popular haunt for customers of

- 🕐 Mon-Sat 11.00-23.00; Sun 12.00-22.30
- 🍴 Good quality, simple pub food
- £ Visa, Mastercard, Delta, Switch
- 🅿 Beer garden
- 🎵 Sunday night pub quiz, pool, darts
- @ sarah-yohah@supanet.com
- ❓ Cissbury Ring 3 miles, The Body Shop Factory Tour 8 miles, Arundel Castle 8 miles, The Wildfowl Trust Arundel 8 miles, Brighton 12 miles

all ages. In the public bar the locals keep the attentive staff nice and busy, while a more relaxed atmosphere can be found in the lounge bar.

To the rear a bright and airy conservatory area is popular in summer, as is the quiet, secluded beer garden. The bar stocks a selection of real ales, together with other popular beers and lagers. Simple, tasty pub food is available every lunchtime with a good variety of options on the menu, all sensibly priced, and with a traditional roast served on Sundays. There is no food available in the evenings. A pool table and darts board help while away a soggy afternoon, and on Sunday nights there is a pub quiz.

SOUTH STREET, CUCKFIELD, WEST SUSSEX RH17 5LB
TEL: 01444 413454

Directions: From the end of the M23, follow the A23 south towards Brighton. After about 6 miles turn left onto the A272 following signs for Cuckfield.

Ye White Harte Inne is a traditional olde worlde English country pub located within the picturesque, characterful town of Cuckfield. Adjoining the local church, there is a pretty enclosed garden with tables and parasols, enjoying fine views over the South Downs and for those that are travelling by car,

there is plenty of car parking to the side and rear. Venturing inside, you will find a cosy, intimate bar with fully seated restaurant, all kept delightfully warm in winter weather with open fires. Here you can enjoy a menu of substantial home-cooked food each lunchtime (except

Monday), all prepared using mainly local produce. Sunday lunchtimes also offer traditional roasts.

The meals offer good value for money, there is a fine selection of daily specials and a tempting choice of home-made desserts. The well stocked bar is cask marque approved and offers some fine bitters together with some popular lagers, malts and wines. The licensee, Andrew Felton, has been a local publican for many years and has a friendly, relaxed attitude while also being very attentive to customer's needs. He arranges a programme of live music, with featured performers usually every other week. There is also a meeting room and separate function hall, which are available for parties. Ring for details.

- Mon-Sat 11.00-15.00, 18.00-23.00; Sun 12.00-15.00, 19.00-22.30
- Substantial, home-cooked meals offering good value for money
- Visa, Mastercard, Delta, Switch
- Beer garden, car parking, meeting room, function room
- Live music every other week
- South of England Showground 5 miles, Bluebell Railway 5 miles, Borde Hill Gardens 2 miles, Sheffield Park House and Gardens 7 miles, Nymans Gardens 2 miles

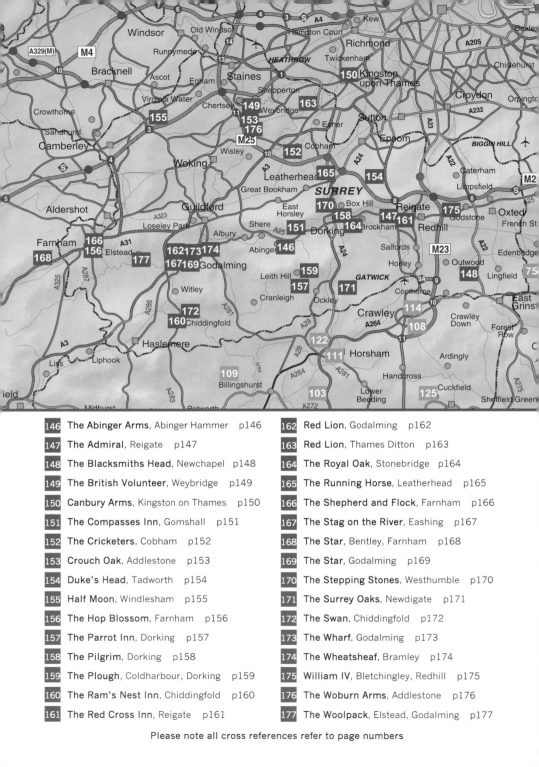

Please note all cross references refer to page numbers

SURREY

Surrey's proximity to the capital and its transport links have defined much of its history. The Thames winds through Surrey to the north of Weybridge and many of the present-day villages and towns developed as riverside trading centres in the medieval period or earlier. Romans marched through this part of Surrey during their conquest of Britain, possibly following the trail of the Celts who were already ensconced there. Saxons left their mark later, bequeathing a number of place names, which duly entered the Domesday Book in the 11th century. The most impressive of all buildings along this - and perhaps any - stretch of the Thames is Hampton Court. Here England's most larger than life monarch acquired and substantially expanded Cardinal Wolsey's palace until it was fit to match his own personality. Later monarchs made their own additions and alterations to both the buildings and the 60 acres of grounds; one of the most popular attractions of all is the famous Maze, planted in 1714. Surrey is full of historical traces. Great houses, as well as royal and episcopal palaces, were built here from medieval times, and many villages have evidence of Saxon, Celtic, Roman and even late Stone Age settlements. The site of one of England's defining moments, the signing of the Magna Carta by King John in 1215 is at the riverside meadow of Runnymede. Here, too, are the Kennedy Memorial, on

Outwood Post Mill

ground given to the people of the USA by the people of Britain; and a shrine to the 20,000 airmen of the Allied Forces who died in World War II and have no known grave. The most impressive of all buildings along the Thames is Hampton Court, where Henry VIII expanded Cardinal Wolsey's already magnificent palace.

History plays an important role in many parts of the county. Civil War battle cries are still almost audible from the walls of Farnham Castle and the hint of plainsong hanging in the still air around the ruins of Waverley Abbey. 'Stand and deliver' would seem to be a more appropriate sound to hear in the wilder sections of the southern extremity, and the Gibbet Memorial on Hindhead Common is a tangible reminder of the fate that awaited those highwaymen who had the misfortune to meet the long arm of the law.

Farnham, with its lovely Georgian architecture and 12th century castle, is the largest town in southwestern Surrey, while Guildford, the ancient county town of Surrey, is an obvious base for travellers interested in exploring Surrey. Guildford has been the capital of the region since pre-Norman times and the remains of Henry II's castle and keep provide commanding views over the surrounding area. The old Georgian cobbled High Street, incorporates the Tudor Guildhall, with its distinctive gilded clock. Woking, like many Surrey towns, was transformed by the arrival of the railway in

Buckland Village

the 19th century. The Victorian influence is evident in many of the larger houses built by Norman Shaw and other proponents of the Arts and Crafts style. The more ornate style of Victorian architecture, designed to reflect the prosperity of a confident imperial power, is also represented in the two massive buildings funded by Thomas Holloway, the Royal Holloway College and the Holloway Sanatorium, which are near Egham in the north. The best of Edwardian architecture is well represented throughout Surrey by the work of Sir Edwin Lutyens, often working in partnership with the eminent gardener Gertrude Jekyll. This famous alliance was responsible for the creation of around 70 gardens between 1893 and 1912, here subtle planting softening and complementing the strong architectural elements of his designs. Lutyens and

Jekyll were both at one time residents of Godalming, and a gallery and garden in the Museum honour this distinguished pair. The timber-framed house once belonging to Gertrude Jekyll can be found in dense woodland on the opposite side of town from the Museum. It was

Polesden Lacey

designed for her by Edwin Lutyens in characteristic rural vernacular style and partially constructed of Bargate stone, a locally quarried hard brown sandstone that was much-loved by the Victorians. The southeast corner of Surrey abuts both Kent to the east and Sussex to the south, and not surprisingly there are elements of both counties in some of the Surrey border villages: Kent weather-boarding features in several of the villages and hamlets near Lingfield.

Its varied architectural heritage belies the notion that Surrey is nothing more than a collection of anonymous suburbs of London. Much of Surrey is indeed the capital's commuter belt and conurbations like Kingston and Croydon spread out into a vast hinterland of suburbia. Woking is a commuter town on the main railway line from Waterloo; the town grew around the station, which when it was built was 2 miles from the old village centre. Brookwood Cemetery, now on the outskirts of town but then in open countryside, was originally built (in 1854) to cope with the problem of finding space for London's dead. The countryside is never far away, and around Guildford and Dorking and near the Sussex border there are small towns and wayside villages amid rough Down and Weald uplands or thickly wooded hillsides. The countryside is varied, from the well-maintained plantation of Kew Gardens, possibly the most famous gardens in the world, to the uplands to the south and numerous parks, greens, heaths, commons and open land. Rich farming areas give way to expanses of heath and woodlands with networks of paths for walkers and cyclists. The famous Hog's Back section of the A31 is one of the most scenic drives in the Southeast, with excellent views north and south as it follows the ridge between Farnham and Guildford through some of Surrey's most unspoilt countryside. The sound of birdsong ringing through the woods or the click of a cricket bat on a village green are as much a part of much of Surrey as the whirring suburban lawnmower.

Abinger

The parish of Abinger contains two villages, Abinger itself (or Abinger Common) which lies one mile west of Friday Street at the southern end of the parish, and **Abinger Hammer** which lies on the A25 Dorking to Guildford road to the north. Abinger claims to be one of the oldest settlements in the country, having been settled by Middle Stone Age people around 5000 BC. The remains of a Mesolithic pit-dwelling were discovered in a field near Abinger's old Manor House, which, when excavated in 1950,

revealed over 1,000 tools and artefacts which are now on display in an interesting little museum.

Abinger Common is a delightful hamlet, and Abinger Hammer was once known for the manufacture of cannon

Jack the Smith Hammer Clock

balls; and a busy blacksmith's workshop can still be found here. Abinger Hammer's industrial past is reflected in the unique Jack the Smith hammer clock, in which the figure of a blacksmith strikes a bell with his hammer every half hour.

Albury

Dating largely from the 19th century, Albury was constructed in fanciful neo-Gothic style as an estate village for nearby **Albury Park**. This large country mansion, which boasts no fewer than 63 chimneys in an amazing variety of shapes and sizes, stands in gardens laid out by the diarist John Evelyn at the turn of the 18th century. The main feature is a series of terraced orchards rising above the house to the north.

Box Hill

The 563 foot Box Hill lies a couple of miles from Polesden Lacey (see under

Great Bookham) on the eastern side of the River Mole. This popular local landmark rises sharply from the valley floor to an impressive tree-covered summit, 400 feet above. The National Trust owns over 800 acres of land around Box Hill which has now been designated a country park. The hillside is traversed by a series of nature walks, and there are also several picnic sites, which enjoy breathtaking views across the Weald to the South Downs.

Brockham

Brockham is a picture-postcard village set around a quintessential three-sided village green on which cricket is played in summer, a Guy Fawkes bonfire is lit in autumn, and Christmas carols are sung in winter. The legendary cricketer WG Grace is even said to have played here. Noteworthy buildings in the village include the late 18th century **Brockham Court**, and the part 17th century Feltons Farm, which lies a short distance away to the southwest. The remains of some 19th century industrial kilns can be seen on the Downs above the village in the disused Brockham Quarries.

Chiddingfold

With its three-sided green, waterlily-filled pond, part 13th century church, medieval pub and

Brockham Village

handsome collection of Georgian cottages, this attractive settlement contains all the features of a quintessential English village. During the 13th and 14th centuries, it was an important centre of the glass-making industry, and some fragments of medieval Chiddingfold glass can be seen in the small lancet window in St Mary's Church.

Cobham

Cobham is home to the **Cobham Bus Museum**, which houses the largest collection of London buses in the world. One mile west of Cobham is **Painshill Park**, a white 18th century house with a fine setting on a hill. The house is impressive but Painshill is more noted for its grounds, which were laid out by the Hon Charles Hamilton, son of the Earl of Abercorn, in the 1740s. These grounds include an ornamental lake in front of a Gothic brick abbey, a Chinese bridge and a waterwheel; Hamilton even

built a hermitage, and then went one stage further by installing a hermit in it.

Croydon

First impressions can be deceiving. Nestling beneath some of the most modern high-rises are some much older buildings, including some brick almshouses built in 1599 and now overshadowed by their modern neighbours. More intriguingly, and certainly worth seeking out, are the remains of the palace that was the summer residence of the Archbishops of Canterbury. The palace was built in the 11th century by Archbishop Lanfranc. It was considerably altered and expanded in subsequent centuries but remained an official residence until 1757. **The Palace** is now part of the Old Palace School for girls but the public can see some of the oldest surviving elements, including the Norman undercroft and the 15th century banqueting hall.

  St John the Baptist Church is the largest parish church in Surrey, with a two-storey porch and fine tower. Its enormous size puts it in a league with St Mary Redcliffe in Bristol and St Martin in Salisbury. The 15th century church burnt down in 1867 but was rebuilt by 1870 on the old foundations in a style that largely matches the earlier church. Some original

Painshill Park

elements of the medieval church remain in the restored tower and the south porch.

Croydon also has a handsome arts complex, the **Fairfield Halls**, which flank one edge of a modern flower-filled square in the heart of Croydon. It comprises a main concert hall, the Peggy Ashcroft Theatre, the Arnhem Art gallery and a general-purpose lounge which doubles as a banqueting hall. **Waddon Caves**, along Alton Road, were the site of late Stone Age and Iron Age settlements, which were inhabited until the 3rd or 4th century AD.

Egham

Between Egham and Englefield Green is one of Surrey's more memorable buildings, the **Royal Holloway College**. It is a huge Victorian building, modelled on the Chateau du Chambord in the Loire Valley in France. Opened by Queen Victoria in 1886, it was one of the first colleges for women in the country. Like the Holloway Sanatorium at Virginia Water, it was designed by WH Crossland for Thomas Holloway. Holloway's generous ideas on lodging - each student was allocated two rooms - dictated the enormous size of the building. In the form of a double quadrangle, it measures 550 feet in length and 376 feet across. Inside, the formal rooms include a remarkable library and a picture gallery, housing a

collection of Victorian paintings by artists such as Millais, Landseer and Frith. Now part of the University of London, the college has a student population of over 4000 and male students have been admitted since 1965.

Elstead

Just west of the centre of this attractive village is **Elstead Mill**, an 18th century water mill. It stands four storeys high, its brick structure topped with a Palladian cupola. Six classical columns support a small lead dome at the very top. It is now a restaurant, with much of the machinery, including a working water wheel, displayed within.

Elstead Mill

Epsom

Epsom's main claim to fame is as a horse racing centre. Each year in early June, the Downs to the southeast of the town take on a carnival atmosphere as tens of thousands of racing enthusiasts come to experience the annual Classic race meeting and the colourful fun fair, which accompanies it. Informal horse racing took place on **Epsom Downs** as long ago as 1683 when Charles II is said to have been in attendance. Racing was formalised in 1779 when a party of aristocratic sportsmen led by Lord Derby established a race for three year old fillies which was named after the Derbys' family home at Banstead, the Oaks; this was followed a year later by a race for all three year olds, the **Derby**, which was named after the founder himself, although only after he won a toss of a coin with the race's co-founder, Sir Charles Bunbury. (Had Lord Derby lost, the race would have become known as the Bunbury.)

Esher

Esher is well known as the home of **Sandown Park**, the world-class racecourse, where horse racing is staged all year round. Nearby, and well worth a visit, is the beautiful National Trust-owned **Claremont Landscape Garden**, begun in 1715 and believed to be one of the earliest surviving examples of an

English landscape garden. Over the years some of the greatest names in garden history including William Kent, Capability Brown, Sir John Vanbrugh and Charles Bridgeman have been involved in its creation. The grounds include a number of striking vistas and contain a grassed amphitheatre, grotto, lake and an island with a pavilion.

Farnham

The most westerly town in Surrey is Farnham, a market town of particular architectural charm with its 12th century castle overlooking Georgian houses in the river valley below. **Farnham Castle** is approached along Castle Street, a delightful wide thoroughfare of Georgian and neo-Georgian buildings which was laid out to accommodate a traditional street market. The old Norman keep, now owned by English Heritage, is open to the public throughout the summer.

The informative **Farnham Museum** is housed in an attractive Grade I Georgian

town house dating from 1718, known as Willmer House in West Street. The house has many original features including a pleasant walled garden at the rear. **Farnham Maltings** in Bridge Square is a thriving arts and community centre housed in a listed early 18th century building. Lying

Farnham Castle

within easy striking distance of Farnham are the atmospheric ruins of Waverley Abbey. Dating from the 12th century, this was the first Cistercian abbey to be built in England. The Abbey remains are open during daylight hours and are said to have provided the inspiration for Sir Walter Scott's romantic novel, *Waverley*.

A lovely riverside walk from Waverley Abbey leads to Tilford, an attractive village which stands at the confluence of the two branches of the River Wey. At the heart of Tilford stands a triangular village green which features a 900-year-old oak tree with a 25 foot girth which is known as the King's or Novel's Oak. Tilford's parish church of All Saints hosts a regular spring festival of early church music. In Reeds Road to the southwest of Tilford is the **Rural Life Centre and Old Kiln Museum**. The writer William Cobbett was the son of a Farnham labourer and is buried beside his father in St Andrew's churchyard.

Godalming

The old market town of Godalming was once an important staging post between London and Portsmouth and a number of elegant 17th and 18th century shops and coaching inns can still be found in the High Street. Perhaps the most interesting building in the old centre is the former town hall, affectionately known as **The Pepperpot**, which was built at the western end of the High

Street in 1814. Now surrounded on all sides by heavy traffic, this unusual arcaded building once contained an interesting museum of local history.

The Museum is now opposite the Pepperpot at the fascinating Wealden House, parts of which date from the 15th and 16th centuries but which also has Victorian and Georgian additions. Godalming's part-Norman parish church of St Peter and St Paul is built of Bargate stone, as is **Charterhouse School**, which moved from London to a hillside site on the northern side of Godalming in 1872. Among its most striking features are the 150 foot Founder's Tower and the chapel designed by Giles Gilbert Scott as a memorial to those killed in the First World War. In the churchyard at Busbridge lies the garden designer Gertrude Jekyll, in a tomb designed by her great friend Sir Edwin Lutyens. Three miles along the B2130 to the southeast of Godalming lies the renowned **Winkworth Arboretum**, a 95 acre area of wooded hillside which was presented to the National Trust in 1952.

Winkworth Arboretum

Godstone

Although Godstone is now thankfully bypassed by the A22, the A25 east-west route still passes through its heart, making a sharp change in direction as it does so. Fortunately, the village's Tudor and Elizabethan character has survived relatively intact. Godstone's most distinguished building, the White Hart Inn in the High Street, claims to have been visited by Richard II, Elizabeth I, Queen Victoria, and even the Tsar of Russia who broke his journey in 1815.

A series of attractive lanes and alleyways connects the High Street to the village green, a broad open space with a cricket pitch, which is surrounded by a wonderful collection of 16th and 17th century buildings, including the Tudor-built Hare and Hounds Inn. Godstone's parish church of St Nicholas is situated half a mile east of the centre and can be reached from the White Hart along an old thoroughfare known as Bay Path. Although Norman in origin, the building was virtually rebuilt in the 1870s by Sir George Gilbert Scott, a local resident at the time. Inside, there is a marble memorial to a cousin of John Evelyn, the famous 17th century diarist. The area around the church contains some fine old buildings, including a row of 19th century almshouses and the 16th century timber-framed Old Pack House, which lies a short distance away to the south. Bay Path also leads to a former hammer pond, **Bay Pond**, which is now a designated nature reserve.

Great Bookham

Great Bookham contains an exceptional parish church, **St Nicholas**, which has an unusual flint tower with a shingled spire dating back to the Norman era in the 12th century. Nearby **Little Bookham** has a small single-roomed church with a wooden belfry that is believed to date from the 12th century. Bookham Common and Banks Common to the northwest of Little Bookham provide some welcome relief from the commuter estates and offer pleasant walking through relatively unspoilt open heathland. Another National Trust-owned property, **Polesden Lacey**, stands on high ground two miles to the south of Great Bookham. The house contains a fine collection of furniture, paintings, tapestries, porcelain and silver, and the surrounding grounds amount to over 1,000 acres and incorporate a walled rose garden, open lawns, a youth hostel and a large area of natural woodland.

Guildford

The route into Guildford from the northwest passes close to **Guildford Cathedral**, one of only two new Anglican cathedrals to have been built in this country since the Reformation (the other is Liverpool). This impressive redbrick building stands on top of Stag Hill, a prominent local landmark which enjoys panoramic views over the surrounding landscape. The building was designed by Sir Edward Maufe with a superb high-arched interior and was

Guildford Castle

grandest 18th century houses in the whole country, it is renowned for its magnificent two-storey marble hall, its fine Italian plasterwork depicting scenes from mythology, and distinguished collections of furniture, porcelain and humorous Meissen figures. The surrounding parkland was designed by Capability Brown.

begun in 1936. However, work was halted during World War II and members of the local diocese had to wait until 1961 for the new cathedral to be finally consecrated. Guided tours and restaurant facilities are available all year round.

In 1968, the **University of Surrey** relocated from London to a site on a hillside to the northwest of the cathedral. Henry II built a **Castle** here on high ground in the 12th century which later became the county gaol. Today, the castle remains and the ruined keep provide a fascinating place from which to view the surrounding area. The Chestnuts, on Castle Hill, was the family home of Lewis Carroll, author of the Alice stories. He is buried in Mount Cemetery, and on the far bank of the River Way is a charming bronze memorial to him, consisting of a life-size Alice chasing the White Rabbit into his hole.

In farming countryside east of Guildford is the National Trust-owned Clandon Park, a splendid Palladian mansion built in about 1730 by Giacomo Leoni, a Venetian architect. One of the

Hampton Court

In 1514 Thomas Wolsey, the Archbishop of York took a 99-year lease on the buildings at Hampton Court. Wolsey created a magnificent residence with new kitchens, courtyards, lodgings, galleries and gardens. Henry VIII comprehensively rebuilt and extended the palace over the following ten years to accommodate his wives, children and court attendants. Although much of Henry VIII's building work has been demolished over the years, the Great Hall and the Chapel Royal survive, the latter still in use as a place of worship.

The Great Hall, which Henry had completed in 1534, having forced the builders to work night and day, has mounted stag heads and fine tapestries lining the walls beneath the intricate hammerbeam roof. It was the scene of theatrical productions during the reigns of Elizabeth I and James I, and among the performing troupes was that of William Shakespeare. Also intact are the enormous Tudor Kitchens, with the huge fireplaces and assortment of ancient cooking utensils that would have been used in the 16th century to prepare a feast fit for a king.

The courtyards and buildings to the left still contain a number of 'grace and favour' apartments, where Crown officials and dependants of the Royal family live. William III and Mary II made the first major alterations to the palace since Tudor times. They commissioned Sir Christopher Wren to rebuild the king's and queen's apartments on the south and east sides of the palace, although the queen's apartments were left unfinished at the queen's death. King William III's Apartments remain one of the most magnificent examples of Baroque state apartments in the world. Almost destroyed in a terrible fire in 1986, there followed an ambitious restoration project which returned the apartments to the way they were when they were completed for William III in 1700. They can now be seen in their original glory, still furnished with the fine furniture and tapestries of 1700. There are over 60 acres of gardens to explore at Hampton Court including the Great Vine, the Privy Garden and the famous **Maze**.

Kew and Kew Gardens

Kew is best known for the **Royal Botanic Gardens**, arguably the most famous gardens in the world. Princess Augusta, mother of George III, laid out an eight acre botanical garden on the grounds of Kew Palace in 1759. Tranquil and spacious, this garden, now extending

over 300 acres, has become an important botanical research centre. Over a million visitors a year are attracted to view the 40,000 species of plants and 9,000 trees which grow here in plantations and glasshouses. The most famous and oldest glasshouse, built in 1848, is the Palm House, which houses most of the known palm species. Nearby is the Water Lily House, full of tropical vines and creepers overhanging its lily pond. The Prince of Wales Conservatory, which opened in 1987, houses plants from ten different climatic zones, from arid desert to tropical rainforest. The co-founder and director of the Gardens, Sir William Jackson Hooker, and his son Sir Joseph Dalton Hooker, who succeeded him, are buried at St Anne's Church, Kew Green. Also here are the tombs of two distinguished painters, Thomas Gainsborough and John Zoffany.

Kingston

The first impression most people have of Kingston is of high-rise office blocks and its famous by-pass, giving it the sense of being totally urbanised and something of a modern creation. However Kingston has been a thriving market town since the Middle Ages, the first of only four Royal Boroughs in England and Wales. **The Guildhall**, built in 1935, is solid and functional, but nearby beside the 12th century Clattern Bridge over the River Hogsmill stands the Coronation Stone, said to have been used in the crowning of up to seven Saxon kings. many medieval monuments. On the London Road is a real medieval relic - the chapel of **St Mary Magdalene**, dating from the 14th century.

Leith Hill

The 965 foot National Trust-owned Leith Hill is the highest point in the southeast of England. In 1766, a 64 foot tower was built on the tree-covered summit by Richard Hull, a local squire who lived at nearby Leith Hill Place. He now lies buried beneath his splendid creation. Present-day visitors climbing to the top on a clear day can enjoy a panorama, which takes in several counties and reaches as far as the English Channel. Leith Hill Place stands within beautiful rhododendron filled grounds, which are open to the public throughout the year.

Limpsfield

The churchyard at Limpsfield, three miles to the east of Godstone, contains the grave of the composer, Frederick Delius, who despite having died in France, left instructions that he should be buried in an English country grave-yard. Also buried here is Sir Thomas Beecham, a great admirer of Delius (he read Delius' funeral oration and con-ducted works by him at the funeral service). Detillens, a rare 15th century 'hall' house, is also located in Limpsfield. This striking building has an unusual king-post roof, and despite having been given a new facade in the 18th century,

is a good example of a house belonging to a Surrey yeoman, a member of the class of small freeholders who cultivated their own land. Inside, there is an interesting collection of period furniture, china and militaria.

Limpsfield Chart, or simply The Chart, constitutes a hilltop common with some lovely views eastwards across Kent. Next to the common is the 17th century Mill House. The windmill itself was removed in 1925. Elsewhere in The Chart there are handsome groupings of stone-built houses, cottages, and farm buildings, best exemplified by the ensemble at Moorhouse Farm.

Lingfield

Lingfield is a large village set within delightful wooded countryside in the southeastern corner of the county. Almost large enough to be called a town, 'leafy Lingfield' is perhaps best known to the world at large for its racecourse. However, the settlement has long been an important agricultural centre, whose largely Perpendicular church of St Peter and St Paul has been enlarged over the centuries to create what has become known as the 'Westminster Abbey of Surrey'. As well as having a rare double nave and an exceptional collection of monumental brasses, the church also contains a surprising number of memori-als to members of the Cobham family, the medieval lords of the manor who lived at the now demolished **Starborough Castle**, a mile and a half to the east.

Greathed Manor, to the southeast of Lingfield, is a substantial Victorian manor house built in 1868 for the Spender Clay family.

Loseley Park

Loseley Park is a handsome Elizabethan country estate built in 1562 of Bargate stone. Both Elizabeth I and James I are known to have stayed at Loseley House, whose interior boasts many outstanding period features, including hand-painted panelling, woodcarving, delicate plasterwork ceilings and a unique chimneypiece carved carved from A massive piece of chalk. The walled garden is a delightful place for a stroll, and the nearby fields are home to Loseley's famous herd of pedigree Jersey cattle.

Ockley

Lots of interest here, starting with a village green which, at over 500 feet in diameter, is one of the largest in Surrey. In summer, village cricket is played in this classic English setting which is enhanced by a number of handsome period houses and cottages. An interesting private sculpture and ceramics gallery, the **Hannah Peschar Gallery-Garden**, which incorporates a delightful water garden, is located a mile southwest of Ockley.

Outwood

Outwood Common, the area of high ground to the east of village, is the site of

Hannah Peschar Gallery Garden

one of the most interesting windmills in the country. **The Post Mill** is acknowledged as the oldest working windmill in England. It was built in 1665 and it is said that from the top of the mill, some 39 feet up, the Great Fire of London was visible 27 miles away. Unlike other ancient buildings in England, the Post Mill's early history is not shrouded in mystery and conjecture. It was built by Thomas Budgen, a miller of Nutfield, and the original deeds are still in existence.

For over a century, a second 'smock' windmill stood nearby, and the pair were known locally as the Cat and Fiddle; sadly, the Fiddle blew down in a storm in the early 1960s.

Oxted

Oxted is an old town that prospered because of its position just below the Downs and consequently a good trading link with the rest of Surrey. Today, however, Oxted constitutes two distinct parts. New Oxted lies between the original town and Limpsfield and grew up around the railway station. Old Oxted is also largely Victorian to the eye, but occasionally the visitor notices some survivors of earlier centuries such as the Forge House and Beam Cottages, with their medieval core and 17th century exteriors. Streeters Cottage, built in the 17th century, presents a large timber-framed gable to the road.

Reigate

Reigate is a prosperous residential town whose expansion at the hands of postwar developers has done much to conceal its long and distinguished history. The settlement was once an important outpost of the de Warenne family, the assertive Norman rulers whose sphere of influence stretched from the Channel coast to the North Downs. As at Lewes, they built a castle on a rise above the village streets of which nothing remains today except for an arch, which was reconstructed in the 1770s from material recovered from the original castle walls. Today, this striking neo-Gothic repro-duction stands at the heart of a pleasant public park. The **Old Town Hall**, a handsome redbrick building constructed in 1729, stands at the eastern end of the

High Street, and a short distance away to the north, the entrance to a disused road tunnel can be seen. This was built beneath the castle mound in 1824 to ease the through-flow of traffic on the busy London to Brighton coaching route. **Reigate Priory**, now a Grade 1 listed building set in 65 acres of parkland, has been remodelled on a number of occasions, in particular during the Georgian era. It now operates as a school and museum. On Reigate Heath stands a church situated in a windmill.

Richmond

A good place to get acquainted with old Richmond is **Richmond Green**, a genuine village green, flanked on the southwest and southeast edges by handsome 17th and 18th century houses. The southwest side has an older, and more royal, history. It was the site of Richmond Palace, built in the 12th century and passing into royal possession in 1125, when it was known as Shene Palace. The palace was destroyed by Richard II in 1394 but subsequent kings had it rebuilt in stages. The site, right by the green, made it an ideal spot for organising jousting tournaments. The rebuilding and extensions reached their peak under Henry VII, who renamed the palace after his Yorkshire earldom. Elizabeth I died in the palace in 1603. Sadly the only surviving element of the palace is the brick gatehouse beside the village green.

Just off the northeast flank of the green is the **Richmond Theatre**, an imposing Victorian building with an elaborate frontage facing the street. It is a showcase for excellent theatrical productions. The combination of the repertoire and the lovely setting attracts a number of renowned actors.

Richmond's Old Town Hall is the home of the **Museum of Richmond**, a fascinating privately run museum which provides a unique perspective on Richmond's history and special significance in English life.

The steep climb of Richmond Hill leads southwards and upwards from the centre of Richmond. The view from Richmond Terrace has been protected by an Act of Parliament since 1902. The Thames lies below, sweeping in majestic curves to the west through wooded countryside. Turner and Reynolds are among the many artists who have tried to capture the essence of this scene, which takes in six counties. A little further up the hill is the entrance to Richmond Park.

Runnymede

A meadow beside the River Thames to the north of Egham is where King John was forced by the barons to sign **Magna Carta** in 1215. The historic Runnymede Site and nearby Cooper's Hill are contained within a 300 acre tract of land which is now under the ownership of the National Trust. The area contains three separate memorials: a domed neoclassical temple which was erected by the American Bar Association to commemorate the sealing of the world's first bill of

democratic rights, a memorial to John F. Kennedy, and the **Air Forces Memorial**. The nearby **Runnymede Pleasure Ground** offers a range of children's leisure activities in a pleasant riverside setting.

Shepperton

Shepperton has capitalised on its strategic riverside location, and grew from its origins as a straggling collection of homesteads to become a bustling way station for west-bound traffic from London. The 20th century brought a new wave of development with the building of **Shepperton Film Studios** in the 1930s. Handy for London's Airport, first at Croydon then at Heathrow, Shepperton presented itself as an ideal site for a film venture. International stars were collected from their transatlantic flights or from their Mayfair flats. Moreover, Shepperton's position at the edge of the Green Belt meant that 'rural' location shots could be managed just a few miles from the studios themselves.

Shere

Shere is one of the loveliest, and consequently most visited, villages in Surrey. The village **Church of St James** dates from the 12th century and was tastefully restored in the 1950s. Among its many noteworthy features are the 13th century Purbeck marble font, the St Nicholas Chapel, and an unusual hermit's cell built in the 14th century for a local woman who asked to be

Shere Village

confined there for life.

The **Shere Museum** in the Malt House contains an interesting collection of local artefacts, and the Old Farm behind the church is an open farm, which, at weekends, offers hands-on demonstrations of traditional farming techniques.

Twickenham

Perhaps more than anything else Twickenham is renowned as the headquarters of Rugby Union Football in Britain, a role it has played since 1907. The recently rebuilt stadium plays host to England home internationals as well as the annual Varsity match between Oxford and Cambridge. The **Museum of Rugby** allows visitors to savour the history and atmosphere of the sport.

Montpelier Row and Sion Row, wonderfully preserved 18th century terraces, are some of the fine old houses in the heart of Twickenham. At **Strawberry Hill**, just to the south of Twickenham, is the villa bought by the

author Horace Walpole in 1749 and remodelled into a 'gothic fantasy', which has been described as 'part church, castle, monastery or mansion'. **Orleans House and Gallery**, which houses one of the finest art collections outside of London's national collections, enjoys an enviable location in a woodland garden on the Riverside between Twickenham and Richmond.

On the opposite riverbank, accessible by passenger ferry for most of the year, is **Ham House**, built in 1610, and then enlarged in the 1670s. Now in the hands of the National Trust, Ham's lavish Restoration interiors and magnificent collection of Baroque furniture provide a suitable setting for the popular summer ghost walks.

Virginia Water

The 'water' in the name is a mile and a half long artificial lake set within mature woodland at the southern end of **Windsor Great Park**; it was created by Paul and Thomas Sandby, two accomplished Georgian landscapers who were also known for their painting. The picturesque ruins standing at the lakeside are genuine remains of a Roman temple which once stood at Leptis Magna in Libya. **The Valley Gardens** also contain an unusual 100 foot totem pole which was erected here in 1958 to mark the centenary of British Columbia. A little further to the north, the Savill Garden is renowned as one of the finest woodland gardens in the country.

Holloway Sanatorium, now renamed **Crossland House**, was designed by the Victorian architect WH Crossland for the eminent businessman and philanthropist Thomas Holloway. It was built to house middle-class people, afflicted with mental disease. Holloway Sanatorium looked to the continent for inspiration, to the architecture of Bruges and Ypres. The result was a brick and stone Gothic structure that stood as the epitome of high Victorian fashion, ironically constructed after the popularity of that overblown style had begun to ebb. This Grade I listed building had fallen into dereliction until 1998, when it was sensitively restored as part of a prize winning housing development at Virginia Park.

Weybridge

The town once possessed a palace, **Oatlands Park**, in which Henry VIII married his fifth wife, Catherine Howard, in 1540; 110 years later, the building was demolished and the stone used in the construction of the Wey Navigation. Weybridge stands at the northern end of this historic inland waterway, which was one of the first examples of its kind when it was completed in 1670. It extends

for almost 20 miles southwards to Godalming and incorporates large sections of the main river.

In 1907, the worlds first purpose-built motor racing track was constructed on the **Brooklands** estate near Weybridge, and in the years which followed, this legendary banked circuit hosted competitions between some of the most formidable racing cars ever made. In recent years, the circuit has undergone something of a revival with the opening of the **Brooklands Museum**, a fascinating establishment centred on the old Edwardian clubhouse, now restored to its pre-war elegance.

Wisley

The Royal Horticultural Society's internationally renowned **Wisley Garden** lies on the north side of the A3, one mile to the northwest of Ockham. As well as containing a wide variety of trees, flowering shrubs and ornamental plants, this magnificent 250 acre garden incorporates the Society's experimental

Wisley Garden

beds where scientific trials are conducted into new and existing plant varieties. Wisley also acts as a centre for training horticultural students, and offers a wide range of plants, books, gifts and gardening advice at its first-class plant centre and shop.

Witley

The historic village of Witley comprises an attractive collection of fine tile-hung and half-timbered buildings loosely arranged around the part-Saxon church of All Saints. The **Old Manor** was visited by a number of English monarchs, including Edward I and Richard II, and the village centre contains some delightful 15th and 16th century timber-framed houses, many of which are hung with characteristic fishtail tiles. At one time, Witley was a summer haven for artists and writers, the best known of which is perhaps George Eliot who wrote her last novel, *Daniel Deronda*, here between 1874 and 1876. **Tigburne Court**, which is regarded by many as Lutyens's finest work, is just over a mile south of Witley, standing right on the main Milford to Petworth road. It was built between 1899 and 1901 for Sir Edgar Horne. The gardens, like those of so many of the best Lutyens houses, are by Gertrude Jekyll.

Woking

Most of the heart of Woking dates from the middle of the 19th century, but among these Victorian-era buildings is an unexpected 'first'. The first purpose-built mosque to be founded in Britain - **Shah Jehan Mosque** - can be found in Woking's Oriental Street. The streets of **Old Woking** contain some noteworthy old buildings, including the 17th century Manor House, and the part-Norman parish church of St Peter, which has a late-medieval west tower. Located roughly midway between Woking and Byfleet is Pyrford, which manages to retain many aspects of its village character despite being no more than a couple of miles from its larger neighbours. It is set in meadows along the River Wey, with most of its original red-brick cottages still forming a core near the church. This parish church, the largely Norman **Church of St Nicholas**, has been preserved over the centuries without being the victim of intrusive restoration work. About half a mile along the B367, to the south of Pyrford, is **Newark Priory**, an evocative ruin set in fields along the banks of the Wey. **Brookwood Cemetery**, just west of Woking, was opened in 1854; it is the largest in the country and once even had its own station - the remains of the platforms can still be seen. Among the many thousands who have found their final resting place in Brookwood are the painter John Singer Sargent, the author Dame Rebecca West and the murderess Edith Thompson. Dodi Fayed's body lay here for a short while before being transferred by his father to the family estate at Oxted. Two miles from Brookwood, in the village of St John's, is Britain's first crematorium.

Surrey

THE ABINGER ARMS

GUILDFORD ROAD, ABINGER HAMMER, SURREY RH5 6RZ
TEL: 01306 730145

Directions: From junction 10 of the M25, take the A3 towards Guildford. After 4 miles turn right onto the A247 and at the junction with the A246 continue straight on to the A25 towards Dorking. Abinger Hammer is then just a further 5 miles.

The Abinger Arms has been managed by local girl Helen Burt for the past six months, and she runs the place with her brother, who is the chef, together with the assistance of their parents. This genuine coaching inn dates back to the 16th century and presents an attractive tiled frontage to passers-by. In

keeping with the characterful frontage, inside you will find a cosy interior with simple furnishings, thoughtfully laid out, and a home from home atmosphere.

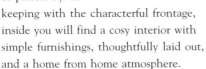

- Mon-Sat 11.00-23.00; Sun 11.00-22.30
- Delicious home-cooked food offering excellent value
- Visa, Mastercard, Delta, Switch
- Beer garden, car park
- Darts nights, monthly live music
- Albury Park 3 miles, Guildford 7 miles, Ranmore Forest Walk 3 miles, Polesden Lacey 5 miles, Box Hill 7 miles, Leith Hill Tower 4 miles, Winkworth Arboretum 11 miles

Here you can enjoy a refreshing drink from the good range at the well stocked bar, which includes some real ales, lager and wines. A tasty selection of food is available from midday until 3pm and in the evening between 6.30pm and 9.30pm. The menu is made up of traditional English dishes, offering beef, poultry, fish and game, with everything being freshly prepared and providing excellent value for money. To round off your meal there is also a superb choice of home-made desserts. The locals indulge in regular darts competitions, and there are occasional race nights and live music once a month.

THE ADMIRAL

109A NUTLEY LANE, REIGATE, SURREY RH2 9EF
TEL: 01737 210856

Directions: The town of Reigate can be found just a couple of miles south of junction 8 of the M25.

The Admiral Inn can be found just a short walk from the centre of the busy residential town of Reigate and is a handsome building, enjoying a corner location. Recently taken over by Jay McKeever, this young landlord already has a popular reputation, having previously run the town's Market Hotel for many years. This is his first venture into running a pub but it is clear that it will become a resounding success.

Catering mainly to the local trade, the bar is open all day every day serving a

selection of traditional real ales together with other popular lagers, beers, ciders, bottled drinks, spirits and wine. To enjoy with your drink there is also a selection of simple bar snacks available from midday until 9pm daily. The range of snacks includes pies, paninis and sandwiches. As the name suggests, the décor has a nautical theme though Jay has plans to bring it more up to date. It will be kept simple, pleasant and bright, while retaining the separate public and lounge bar areas and the open log fire. There are plenty of tables and cosy corners in which to enjoy a quiet drink, but for a more lively evening there is live music provided once a month. Ring ahead for details.

🕐 Mon-Sat 12.00-23.00; Sun 12.00-22.30

🍴 Simple bar snacks served all day

🎵 Live music monthly, darts, pool table

@ julian.mckeever@btopenworld.com

❓ Box Hill 6 miles, Polesden Lacey 8 miles, Epsom Downs Racecourse 6 miles, Gatwick Airport 6 miles, Holmwood Common 6 miles

THE BLACKSMITHS HEAD

NEWCHAPEL ROAD, NEWCHAPEL, NR. LINGFIELD, SURREY RH7 6LE
TEL/FAX: 01342 833697

Directions: From junction 6 of the M25 take the A22 south towards East Grinstead. After about 4 miles, with the Mormon Temple ahead, turn left at the roundabout on the B2028 signposted for Lingfield. The pub is 200 yards on the left.

The Blacksmiths Head was purpose built in 1924 on the site of an old smithy. The present owners have extensively refurbished it over the last four years. The pub offers a traditional welcome and is conveniently located on the Sussex/Surrey borders just 15 minutes from Gatwick airport.

The interior is open plan and well designed, with a non-smoking restaurant adjoining the bar areas. Real ales served include a number of small independent breweries, with some local to the area. All are well kept and the pub has won awards for its cellar craft and features in the Good Beer Guide. Food is served each lunchtime and evening with a wealth of selection from the menus and daily specials all served by attentive staff at sensible prices.

A real highlight of the Blacksmiths Head is the luxurious accommodation that is newly available. There are five superbly appointed guest rooms with four enjoying en-suite facilities and the other having a private bathroom. Beautifully decorated and furnished, this would make a delightful place to stay before flying out from Gatwick or as a touring base to the many delightful stately homes and gardens. A real treat!

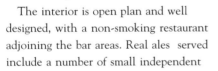

🕐 Mon-Fri 11.00-15.00, 17.30-23.00; Sat 12.00-15.00, 18.00-23.00; Sun 12.00-22.30

🍴 Honest, home-cooked dishes

💷 Visa, Mastercard, Delta, Switch, Amex

🛏 Five luxury rooms

🅿 Landscaped gardens, beer garden, car park

❓ Lingfield Racecourse 3 miles, Gatwick Airport 6 miles, Hever Castle 9 miles, Chartwell 11 miles. Standen, Ashdown Forest, Nymans Gardens, Wakehurst Gardens, Sheffield Park Gardens all within easy reach

THE BRITISH VOLUNTEER

HEATH ROAD, WEYBRIDGE, SURREY KT13 8TH
TEL: 01932 847733   FAX: 01932 858300

Directions: From junction 10 on the M25 take the A3 towards Esher. At the first roundabout turn left on to the A245 then right onto the B374, past Brooklands Museum, and into Weybridge.

Built in the late 19th century, **The British Volunteer** is an eye-catching late Victorian inn that is bedecked by flower filled hanging baskets, window boxes and tubs throughout the year. Probably named after General Kitchener's recruitment campaign during the First World War, the inn's distinctive pub sign is taken from those early 20th century posters, however no one need feel under any pressure to enter this superb pub other than for food and drink. In the large and comfortable bar area customers can enjoy a drink from the well stocked bar where not only are there several real ales but there is also Guinness, served extra cold, and wine lovers can indulge themselves in the

comprehensive list. The bar snacks and meals are also tempting and, as well as the mouth-watering selection of sandwiches and baguettes, the chef also offers a number of interesting and ethnic alternatives. The attractive conservatory restaurant serves from a more substantial eclectic menu. It can also be used for private functions.

Run by experienced licensee Carol Curry, with the help of her husband, sports journalist and broadcaster Steve Curry, the newest addition Victoria Cottage, a bed and breakfast, which is adjacent to the pub. Here there are four comfortable guest rooms available, each attractively furnished and provided with tea and coffee making facilities. The bedrooms share two good-sized bathrooms, and rates are reasonable, making this an ideal overnight stopping place.

- 🕐 Mon-Thur 11.00-15.00, 17.30-23.00; Fri, Sat, Sun all day
- 🍴 Bar meals and snacks, a la carte
- £ Visa, Access, Delta, Switch, Diners
- 🛏 4 rooms sharing 2 bathrooms
- Ⓟ Beer garden, limited car parking, functions catered for
- 🎵 Disco Sunday, pool, darts
- ❓ Brooklands Motor Museum 1 mile, Claremont Landscape Garden 4 miles, Sandown Park Racecourse 4 miles, R.H.S. Wisley Gardens 5 miles, Hampton Court Palace 6 miles

Surrey

THE CANBURY ARMS

49 CANBURY PARK ROAD, KINGSTON UPON THAMES,
SURREY KT2 6LQ
TEL/FAX: 0208 288 1882

Directions: From junction 10 on the M25 follow the A3 then the A240 into the heart of Kingston Upon Thames.

Built in 1888, **The Canbury Arms** is an eye-catching corner inn that has a distinctive white painted front façade. The exterior is adorned with colourful hanging baskets and it has the air of being a busy, friendly town centre pub, conveniently located for shoppers and tourists. This splendid drinking establishment has been

managed by Paul Adams since 1988 and it is easy to see that it is his hard work and friendly personality, together with a passion for music, that have made this into the popular inn you see today.

Very much a pub for regular

- 🕐 Mon-Sat 11.00-23.00; Sun 12.00-22.30
- 💷 Visa, Mastercard, Delta, Switch
- Ⓟ Patio garden, car park
- 🎵 Live music Friday and Saturday evenings, pub games
- @ padams.canbury@blueyonder.co.uk
- ❓ Hampton Court 2 miles, Ham House 2 miles, Kew Gardens 4 miles, Sandown Park Racecourse 4 miles, Chessington Zoo 4 miles, Polesden Lacey 12 miles

customers, and enjoying a mixed clientele, this is just the place for a quiet drink and some enjoyable conversation. The walls of the bar are covered with over 400 pump clips and is a reminder that, in the last three years, there have been over 400 guest ales served here. It is easy to see how the pub managed to get through so many - there are always six standard real ales on tap, four of which regularly change. Cider is served here too and every year, at Easter, The Canbury Arms hosts a real cider festival with over 20 different brews to sample. This is a lively pub with a warm and welcoming atmosphere – well worth trying if you're in the area.

THE COMPASSES INN

STATION ROAD, GOMSHALL, GUILDFORD, SURREY GU5 9LA
TEL: 01483 202506

Directions: Leave the M25 at junction 9 and head directly into Dorking. Here, turn right onto the A25 Guildford road and you will find the village of Gomshall after about 6 miles.

The Compasses is a splendid old coaching inn dating back to the early 19th century which has been much extended, in all directions, over the passing years. When it was first opened, the pub's name was 'God Emcompasses', however it was mispronounced so frequently it was eventually changed. Seen at its best in summer, the outside becomes a colourful profusion of flowers with numerous hanging baskets covering almost every inch of the walls. The superb gardens are also enjoyed at their best at this time of year, though they are popular whenever the weather is nice enough for sitting outside. A unique feature is the stream that runs between the pub and the seating area, but a couple of bridges ensure that you don't get your feet wet! Don't be surprised if you happen to spot a couple of ducks following you into the bar either.

Open all day, one of the reasons the place is so popular is that a great menu of home-cooked dishes is available from 12 noon until 9pm, seven days a week and there is a separate, non-smoking dining area for which bookings can be taken. To complement your meal the well-stocked bar offers a choice of traditional real ales and an enjoyable range of wines. There is also en-suite bed and breakfast accommodation available with each room provided with a colour TV and tea and coffee making facilities.

- 🕐 Mon-Sat 11.00-23.00; Sun 12.00-22.30
- 🍴 Excellent, home-cooked menu served all day
- £ Visa, Mastercard, Delta, Switch
- 🛏 3 guest rooms with 2 en-suite
- Ⓟ Beer garden, nearby parking
- ♫ Live music each Friday
- ❓ Albury Park 1 mile, Polesden Lacey 5 miles, Ranmore Forest Walk 4 miles, Guildford 7 miles, Hatchlands Park 4 miles, Clandon Park 4 miles, Winkworth Arboretum 9 miles

THE CRICKETERS

DOWNSIDE, COBHAM, SURREY KT11 3NX
TEL: 01932 862105 FAX: 01932 868186

Directions: From junction 10 on the M25 take the A3 towards London and then first right onto the A245 and follow signs to Cobham. Downside Bridge Road is just off the high street.

The Cricketers is an extremely attractive and well maintained country inn that appears surprisingly rural and secluded even though it lies within easy reach of the M25. The original building dates back to around 1538 although it wasn't recorded as a hostelry until the mid-19th century. The Cricketers overlooks both Downside Common and the village green and boasts a freshly painted black and white frontage and presenting a delightful image that would not look out of place on a chocolate box. A quaint old place, full of atmosphere and charm, the interior of the inn is a mass of low

oak beams, crooked walls and open log fires combined with simple yet comfortable country furnishings. Owned and run by business partners James Clifton and Wendy Luxford, this award-winning pub should not be missed.

Although the bar serves an excellent range of real ales, wines and all the usual beverages, it is the splendid food served here that has placed The Cricketers firmly on the culinary map of Surrey. Naturally, all the dishes are freshly prepared and cooked to order and the menu is one that is sure to excite the most jaded of palettes. There is a menu of bar meals and snacks available while in the restaurant you can enjoy an à la carte menu of tempting and imaginative dishes that are superbly prepared and presented.

- 🕐 Mon-Sat 11.00-14.30, 18.00-23.00; Sun 12.00-19.00 (12.00-22.30 Apr-Sept)
- 🍺 Bar menu, a la carte
- £ Visa, Access, Delta, Switch, Amex, Diners
- Ⓟ Large beer garden, ample car parking, functions catered for
- @ jamesclifton@msn.com
- ❓ Wisley Gardens 3 miles, Brooklands Motor Museum 3 miles, Newark Priory 4 miles, Sandown Park Racecourse 4 miles, Chessington Zoo 4 miles

CROUCH OAK

138 STATION ROAD, ADDLESTONE, SURREY KT15 2BE
TEL: 01932 842562 FAX: 01932 853411

> **Directions:** Leave the M25 at junction 11 and follow signs to Weybridge. At the second roundabout turn right into Station Road.

Dominating Station Road, **The Crouch Oak** in Addlestone offers superb traditional facilities. Originally built in the 1860's, this impressive building boasts a newly refurbished modern interior, with comfortable leather couches within spacious seating areas. Open all day every day, friendly staff welcome their visitors and regulars alike.

The lunch and evening menu's range from an array of mouth-watering sandwiches through to freshly prepared home cooked meals, supplemented by popular daily specials at reasonable prices.

- 🕐 Mon-Thur 11.00-23.00; Fri 11.00-01.00; Sat 11.00-23.00; Sun 12.00-22.30
- 🍴 Traditional pub food
- 💷 Visa, Mastercard, Delta, Switch
- 🛏 Four en-suite rooms
- 🅿 Function room
- 🎵 Karaoke Wednesday and Saturday, Club night Friday, pool table
- ❓ Brooklands Motor Museum 3 miles, R.H.S. Wisley Garden 4 miles, Kempton Park Racecourse 7 miles, Runnymede 6 miles, Thorpe Park 4 miles

Customers can enjoy a variety of entertainment throughout the year; karaoke is forever popular on Wednesday and Saturday evenings and the bar is open until 1am at weekends.

The Crouch Oak also claims a function suite catering for business meetings, conferences and private parties. Facilities include a wide screen T.V., internet connection, video player, flipchart and pens and overhead projector.

Overnight accommodation is available; all rooms are prepared daily and equipped with colour T.V. and tea and coffee making faciliteis.

There is safe parking, easy access to and from the main highways and it is just a two minute walk from the railway station.

DUKE'S HEAD

DORKING ROAD, TADWORTH, SURREY KT20 5SU
TEL: 01737 812173 FAX: 01737 216468

Directions: From the M25 take the A217 at junction 8 and head towards London. After a couple of miles follow signs to Tadworth to the left.

Dating from the 18th century, the **Dukes Head** is an old coaching inn that has the feel of a genuine country pub, making it hard to believe that it is just a stone's throw from the M25. The classic style of the exterior is continued within, and here you will find many of the original features of the building have been retained,

including the open fires and a fine, stone slab floor. In a careful blend of old and new, the place has been totally refurbished and tastefully furnished with large leather couches in the main bar and elegant concealed lighting throughout.

🕐 Mon-Sat 11.00-23.00; Sun 12.00-22.30

🍴 Superb cuisine with an international flavour

£ Visa, Mastercard, Delta, Switch, Amex

ⓟ Disabled toilets, beer garden, car park

@ dukeshead@hotmail.com

❓ Epsom Downs Racecourse 1 mile, Chessington Zoo 5 miles, Box Hill 6 miles, Nutfield Priory 8 miles, Polesden Lacey 9 miles, Hampton Court Palace 11 miles

Attracting a wide ranging clientele, the pub is often frequented by local, wealthy socialites and celebrities. It is clear what everyone comes for though, and that is the superb food and wine. The menu offers a fine selection of dishes inspired by world cuisine, all freshly cooked and fabulously presented – designed to tantalise every tastebud. The same superb selection of dishes is available each lunchtime and evening, with food available until 8.30pm on a Sunday. To complement your meal, or simply to enjoy on its own, then why not sample the extensive wine selection. The list is impressive, with selections from every continent, and all available by the glass or the bottle. Yours hosts are Nick and Anna, business partners, who have made the move from the City and have shown a real flair for the hospitality industry. They will clearly go far.

HALF MOON

CHURCH ROAD, WINDLESHAM, SURREY GU20 6BN
TEL: 01276 473329 FAX: 01276 452023

Directions: The village of Windlesham lies not far from the M3 and can be reached by taking junction 3 and heading towards Bracknell on the A322. Immediately pick up the A30 Staines road and then turn right onto the B386 where the village will be reached after just a mile.

The Half Moon is a sizeable, country inn built by the Sturt family in 1904 and still run by family members, Conrad Sturt and his mother Helga, today. Built at the turn of the century it was expertly designed and has been well maintained by successive generations of the family. With the outside attractively bedecked by flowers, there is also a superb garden with large children's play area. The arched entrance, with a church seat, leads directly into the main bar which is traditionally furnished with chunky

🕐	Mon-Sat 11.00-15.00, 18.00-23.00; Sun 12.00-15.00. 19.00-22.30
🍽	Simple, mouth-watering dishes.
💷	Visa, Mastercard, Delta, Switch, Amex
🅿	Children's play area, beer garden, large car park, disabled toilets
@	conradsturt@msn.com
❓	Guildford 11 miles, Ascot 4 miles, Windsor Safari Park 8 miles, Windsor Castle 10 miles, Runnymede 8 miles, Lightwater Country Park 2 miles

tables and chairs, with a second, long narrow bar leading off to one side. Two open fires keep out the winter chills and an added bonus is the fact that there is no juke box or noisy pub games to spoil your visit. All together there are usually about eight real ales kept on tap, and it is not surprising to learn that Conrad is a true connoisseur of fine ales and the pub features in the Good Beer Guide.

Food is served lunchtime and evening each day, except for Sunday evening, with a menu offering plenty of choice from sandwiches to hearty traditional dishes, all simple yet mouth-watering and sensibly priced. All the ingredients are sourced from local producers who share the same high standards.

THE HOP BLOSSOM

LONG GARDEN WALK, FARNHAM, SURREY GU9 7HX
TEL: 01252 710770 FAX: 01252 711173

Directions: From junction 5 of the M3, take the A287 into the heart of Farnham.

The Hop Blossom is not far from Farnham town centre and yet its quiet location has the feel of being miles away from any busy areas. Built in the 18th century, the attractive hostelry has a long history of serving fine ales and tasty food to the locals, and in recent years has become well known to visitors to the area as well. The main bar areas are cosy and compact with the oak floors, open log fires adding to the traditional feel. A more recent addition is the new conservatory which is crammed full of plants and pots and provides a quiet haven in which to enjoy your drink or a meal.

The pub enjoys a fine reputation for serving fine food, which is not surprising when you learn that not only is the owner, Jim McDonald-Good, a fully qualified chef, but he also employs a full-time chef too. Together they create a superb selection of simple, but inventive dishes, all freshly prepared and cooked to order. Food is available midday until 2.30pm at lunchtime and from 5pm until 10.30pm in the evening, Monday to Friday. On Saturday food is available all day while on Sundays food is only served at lunchtime. With over 70 covers in all, there is usually room to be found, and although everything looks and sounds delicious, the home-made curries are especially highly recommended.

🕐 Mon-Fri 12.00-14.30, 17.00-23.00; Sat 12.00-23.00; Sun 12.00-14.30, 19.00-22.30

🍽 Simple pub food cooked to order

🎵 Live Jazz Thursdays

❓ Farnham Castle, Waverley Abbey 1 miles, Bird World 3 miles, Jenkyn Place Gardens 4 miles, Farnborough 5 miles, Loseley House 8 miles, Guildford 10 miles

THE PARROT INN

FOREST GREEN, NR. DORKING, SURREY RH5 5RZ
TEL: 01306 621339 FAX: 01306 621255

Directions: From junction 9 of the M25 follow the A24 due south, around Dorking and beyond. Four miles south of Dorking, at the roundabout at Beare Green, turn right onto the A29 and after another 3 miles turn right again onto the B2126. Forest Green is then just another 2 miles on the right.

At the foot of Leith Hill, overlooking a large expense of village green and cricket pitch, you will find the 300 year old **Parrot Inn**. Over the centuries, the hostelry has become the sizeable, popular establishment you can see today, surrounded by woodlands and exclusive residential properties. A great deal of the original features have been retained including the stone floors, huge open fires and solid oak beams. The interior is spacious and has clearly been refurbished in recent years with no expense spared.

In the relaxed, comfortable bars, you

can enjoy some fine real ales and an excellent wine list, though it is the delicious food that attracts most customers. The superb menu is served from 11.30am until 9.30pm Monday to Saturday and at lunchtime and in the evening on Sunday. An accomplished chef prepares all the sensational dishes which include beef, game, seafood and ever-changing specials.

A previous owner of the pub was the lead singer from Procul Harum, though it is now run by Jim Ness on behalf of a local businessman. A native of Edinburgh, Jim, has previously run a number of pubs in London and, as well as keeping The Parrot Inn under control, also runs the nearby Forest Green House, a luxurious 10-bedroomed guest house where you can enjoy more of the superb hospitality.

- 🕐 Mon-Sat 11.00-23.00; Sun 12.00-22.30
- 🍴 Sensational food from an accomplished chef
- £ Visa, Mastercard, Delta, Switch, Amex
- 🛏 Nearby, separate 10-bedroomed guest house
- Ⓟ Large beer garden, car park, superb function suite
- @ e-mail: manager@parrot-inn.com website: www.parrot-inn.com
- ❓ Leith Hill Tower 2 miles, Guildford 11 miles, Gatwick Airport 11 miles, Winkworth Arboretum 9 miles

Surrey

THE PILGRIM

STATION ROAD, DORKING, SURREY RH4 1HF
TEL/FAX: 01306 889951

Directions: The town of Dorking lies just 6 miles due south of junction 9 of the M25, following the A24.

On the outskirts of the town of Dorking, located close to Dorking West rail station, is **The Pilgrim**. Enjoying an elevated position, the 17th-century hostelry takes its name from the town's location on the ancient Pilgrim's Way which at one time ran through the town. Presenting an attractive frontage, adorned in summer months by colourful hanging baskets and flowering tubs, this is a popular local hostelry where new customers are always made to feel very welcome. The cosy interior features a public bar and lounge/dining area with oak floors and an open fire adding to the traditional feel, and many visitors return again and again, once they've sampled the food. It will

therefore come as no surprise to learn that that owner, Richard Standen, is a chef and in his four years here has created something of a reputation for fine dining. The menu present mainly classic dishes ranging from bar snacks to delicious hot meals using only the finest locally sourced meat and fresh vegetables. Whether you decide to try a simple sandwich, or the highly recommended roast shoulder of lamb, you can also be assured of great value for money. Food is available each lunchtime and evening Monday to Saturday and the traditional Sunday lunch is served from midday until 5pm.

Comfortable bed and breakfast accommodation is available here with five guest rooms of varying sizes, with twins, a double and a family-sized room available.

- Mon-Sat 11.00-23.00; Sun 12.00-22.30
- Home-cooked menu of bar snacks, lunches and evening meals
- Visa, Mastercard, Delta, Switch
- Five rooms of varying sizes
- Beer garden, car park
- Pool table
- Box Hill 2 miles, Polesden Lacey 2 miles, Ranmore Forest Walk 2 miles, Epsom Downs Racecourse 8 miles, Leith Hill Tower 5 miles, Guildford 12 miles

THE PLOUGH

COLDHARBOUR LANE, COLDHARBOUR, DORKING, SURREY RH5 6HD
TEL: 01306 711793

Directions: From junction 9 of the M25 take the A24 due south into Dorking.
From the centre of the town you will find a minor road signposted to Coldharbour,
just over 3 miles

Surrounded by beautiful National Trust
land in the picturesque village of
Coldharbour, the **Plough Inn** dates back
to the 17th century, when it was originally
a coaching inn, supplying the needs of
travellers. Anna and Rick Abrehart, who
took over in 1989, have continued the
centuries-old tradition of warmth,
hospitality and friendly service, catering
to the needs of modern travellers as well
as local people. The historic inn retains
much of its original character with old
oak floors, solid wooden furniture, and a
pretty restaurant laid out with beautiful
white linen and candles.

Those who appreciate good ale will find
it here, brewed on the premises in the
Leith Hill Brewery, set up by Rick in
1996. The ales are brewed in the
traditional way using only natural
ingredients and are available in the bar
and unique to the Plough Inn.

It's worth a detour to sample the beer
alone but the food is of an equally high
standard. Food is served in the restaurant,
bar or garden, and Rick and Anna are
meticulous about using only fresh, high
quality ingredients. With a superb menu
ranging from gourmet dishes to traditional
English fayre the food is exciting and
varied and attracts diners from all over
Surrey and beyond.

The Plough is in an ideal centre from
which to explore the lovely surrounding
countryside and the inn has six en-suite,
five double and one single, with a further
two sharing a bathroom. Each is
decorated in an individual style, simple
but tasteful, with all the facilities you
would expect in a top quality hotel.

🕐 Mon-Sat 11.00-23.00; Sun 12.00-
22.30

🍴 Exceptional dishes from all over the
world

£ Visa, Mastercard, Delta, Switch

🛏 Eight rooms, six en-suite

Ⓟ Beer garden, car park, function
room

@ theploughinn@btinternet.com

? Leith Hill Tower 1 mile, Gatwick
Airport 11 miles, Albury Park 8
miles, Guildford 13 miles, Nutfield
Priory 10 miles

Surrey

THE RAM'S NEST INN

PETWORTH ROAD, CHIDDINGFOLD, SURREY GU8 4SS
TEL: 01428 644460

Directions: Leaving the M25 at junction 10, follow the A3 towards Guildford and beyond. At Milford turn left onto the A283 and Chiddingfold is then just 4 miles. You will find the Pub 1½ miles south of the Village.

The Ram's Nest Inn is a most attractive 18th century hostelry which enjoys a prime site, set well back from the road and surrounded by beautiful gardens. To the front, in addition to plenty of car parking, there is a beautiful veranda area, covered in wisteria and an enviable spot on a summer's evening.

Venturing inside, the tasteful décor reflects the period of the building with top quality furnishings used throughout. The high standards are a reflection of the hard work that has been put in by the owners Jason and Abbie Baker in the 18 months they have been here, and the inn now enjoys a far reaching reputation for high quality ales, good food and a friendly and relaxed ambiance.

Top quality chefs present a broad based menu of home-made dishes, with the menus being changed regularly to make the most of seasonal produce. The same superb menu of snacks and hot dishes is available lunchtime and in the evening, seven days a week. To enjoy with your meal, the bar stocks a selection of superb cask ales, with the Greene King IPA being a popular choice. To make your visit extra memorable, why not take advantage of the comfortable bed and breakfast accommodation that is available. There are three delightful rooms, each with en-suite facilities, situated in the beautiful gardens to the rear of the pub.

🕐 Mon-Fri 11.00-15.00. 18.00-23.00; Sat 11.00-23.00; Sun 12.00-22.30

🍽 Wide ranging menu available daily

💷 Visa, Mastercard, Delta, Switch

🛏 3 en-suite rooms

🅿 Beer garden, large car park

@ jason@ramsnest669.fsnet.co.uk

❓ Winkworth Arboretum 7 miles, Hascombe Court Gardens 6 miles, Thursley Nature Reserve 6 miles, Guildford 8 miles, Albury Park 12 miles

THE RED CROSS INN

96 HIGH STREET, REIGATE, SURREY RH2 9AP
TEL: 01737 225352 FAX: 01737 225398

Directions: The town of Reigate can be found just a couple of miles south of junction 8 of the M25.

Michael and Susan Bowler took over **The Red Cross Inn** just a year ago and have in that time restored the hostelry to its former popularity. The building has been refurbished inside and out and the local customers have returned in force. Located at one end of Reigate's High Street, the pub dates back to the 14th century

and retains much of its historic character with features including lead paned windows, the original oak floors, stone faced walls and exposed wooden beams. The whole place has clearly been lovingly maintained over the years and there is a genuinely welcoming atmosphere. The

furnishings are in keeping with the overall feel, with the open fires complemented by old leather couches and wooden tables and chairs.

The bar offers a wide range of liquid refreshment with the real ale fans being able to choose from a selection of four. Food is available each lunchtime and weekday evenings (no food Saturday or Sunday nights) and the menu comprises traditional English dishes and more adventurous options, with the freshness of the ingredients and value for money being the prime concerns. There is a regularly updated board offering 'specials with a difference' and each Wednesday night there is a Mexican theme to the menus.

🕐 Mon-Sat 11.00-23.00; Sun 12.00-22.30

🍴 Traditional and more adventurous dishes served

£ Visa, Mastercard, Delta, Switch

@ Michael@bowler8945.fsnet.co.uk

? Holmwood Common 6 miles, Box Hill 6 miles, Epsom Downs Racecourse 6 miles, Gatwick Airport 6 miles, Polesden Lacey 8 miles

Surrey

RED LION

1 MILL LANE, GODALMING, SURREY GU7 1HF
TEL: 01483 415207 FAX: 01483 860102

Directions: Leaving the M25 at junction 10, take the A3 south west to Guildford. In the centre of Guildford pick up the A3100 which will lead you directly to Godalming.

Located just off the High Street, in a prime town centre site, the **Red Lion** is Godalming's original coaching inn, located midway between Portsmouth and London. With a history extending back to the 15th century, most of what you see today was added in the 18th century, with the Games Room Bar originally being the Oddfellow's Hall and the public bar at one time being the town's Grammar School. Probably the largest pub in the town, the pub has been well maintained and recently repainted outside. Inside you will find a well thought out layout with traditional décor, the tables and chairs have been arranged to ensure comfort and intimacy while the atmosphere is relaxed and welcoming.

Your experienced hosts are Ian and Amanda Thomson, who also own another inn in the town.

The bar is well stocked with some fine real ales and the quality has been recognised with an entry in the CAMRA Good Beer Guide since 1994. This is the only public house in the area to offering a variety of independent brewers cask beers, some being very reasonably priced. To complement the beers, there is an excellent menu of home-cooked meals served every lunchtime and Tuesday to Sunday evenings. Again, these are sensibly priced and prepared using the freshest ingredients available from local suppliers. There is a large beer garden with patio area at the back, and in warm weather this is a popular spot in which to take your meal and a drink.

- 🕐 Mon-Sat 11.00-23.00; Sun 12.00-22.30
- 🍴 Fresh, home-made dishes offering good value
- 💷 Visa, Mastercard, Delta, Switch
- 🅿 Beer garden, patio
- 🎵 Beer Festival at Easter and Whitsun, pool table
- @ bestpubbloke@aol.com
- ❓ Loseley House 2 miles, Thursley Nature Reserve 5 miles, Winkworth Arboretum 3 miles, Guildford 4 miles, Albury Park 7 miles, Waverley Abbey 9 miles

RED LION

85 HIGH STREET, THAMES DITTON, SURREY KT7 0SF
TEL: 0208 398 8662

Directions: From junction 10 of the M25 take the A3 towards Kingston Upon Thames. After about 5 miles turn left onto the A244, then right onto the A307. Thames Ditton will then be signposted to the left.

If you like a traditional, homely feel to a pub, then you need look no further than **The Red Lion** in Thames Ditton. Dating back to the 1860s, it retains much of its historic character and presents an attractive frontage to the road, enhanced with colourful hanging baskets in the summer months. Inside it is a real home from home, with the décor pleasing to the eye and kept clean and neat by the highly attentive staff.

There is a comfortable main bar, with a selection of 5 real ales, local and nationally brewed. There is a narrow public bar and an adjoining conservatory restaurant, which is in keeping with the relaxed surroundings, leading to an 18th century walled patio feature garden. Here they can seat up to 50 diners and this area is dedicated non-smoking. A fine menu of traditional English cuisine is offered at lunchtimes, and from 6pm until 10pm, Wednesday to Saturday. On Sunday, a traditional roast lunch is served from midday until 5pm. All meals are freshly prepared and offer good value for money. Run by Tristan and Jacky Underwood, it is Tristan who masterminds the kitchen while Jacky, a former teacher, keeps a watchful eye on the bar. The friendly service attracts a wide ranging clientele with families and children made most welcome. There is a regular quiz night held once a month with supper. Ring for full details.

- 🕐 Mon-Sat 11.00-23.00; Sun 12.00-22.30
- 🍴 Non-smoking conservatory restaurant
- 💷 Visa, Mastercard, Delta, Switch
- 🅿 Beer garden
- 🎵 Monthly quiz nights
- @ tristanunderwood@yahoo.co.uk
- ❓ Sandown Park Racecourse 1 mile, Hampton Court Palace 1 mile, Richmond Park 5 miles, Chessington Zoo 5 miles, Kew Gardens 8 miles, Kempton Park Racecourse 4 miles

THE ROYAL OAK

CHART LANE SOUTH, STONEBRIDGE, DORKING, SURREY RH5 4DJ
TEL: 01306 885420

Directions: Leave the M25 at junction 9 and follow the A24 due south to Dorking.
Continue around the town and you will find Stonebridge signposted off to the left.

Originally a built as a cottage in the early 17th century and then used as a tax collector's office, in the 1800s it was converted to a public house and recorded as "a low class inn for tramps and thieves"! Thus reads the provenance of **The Royal Oak** which can be found on the southern outskirts of Dorking overlooking open farmland. Low ceilings, oak beams, a warm open fire and wood panelling make this a welcoming and cosy place for a drink or traditional bar meal, made clear by today's mixed and

regular clientel.

The separate restaurant area is light and airy with its own bar and French doors that open on to the pretty gardens. The chef has built up a fine reputation for the quality of the food with the menu offering traditional English dishes together with some more unusual options. Of all the choices though, the lamb shank is probably the most popular selection.

The well-stocked bar offers some real ales together with a selection of the usual lagers, beers and ciders. The landlord, Andy Hay, has kept the welcoming atmosphere of a traditional country pub. Well worth a visit.

- 🕐 Mon-Sat 11.00-23.00; Sun 12.00-22.30
- 🍴 Reputation for high quality cuisine
- £ Visa, Mastercard, Delta, Switch
- Ⓟ Children's play area, beer garden, car park
- @ andy@royaloakdorking.co.uk
- ❓ Polesden Lacey 4 miles, Box Hill 4 miles, Guildford 12 miles, Leith Hill Tower 5 miles, Gatwick Airport 7 miles, Nutfield Priory 8 miles

THE RUNNING HORSE

38 BRIDGE STREET, LEATHERHEAD, SURREY KT22 8BL
TEL: 01372 372081 FAX: 01372 386029

> **Directions:** The town of Leatherhead can be found just on the southern side of junction 9 of the M25.

The Running Horse is a deceptively large and spacious pub, conveniently located not far from the town centre and provided with a car park, making it ideal for those passing through the area by car. Dating back to 1403, the hostelry is soon to celebrate its 600 year birthday, yet it is bearing up well. Steve and Emma have been at the helm for the past three years and in their time here have firmly established the pub as a popular eating and drinking place for the discerning customer. Together with their efficient and loyal

staff they look forward to welcoming all visitors, old and new.

Within the cosy, characterful interior there are three distinct areas; a public bar with pool table, a spacious lounge and a dining area. Well known for its fine, real ales, the bar is kept well-stocked with a selection of Youngers Ales on tap. There is a reasonable selection of tasty, home-made pub fayre served with no frills and priced to suit every pocket.

All the meals are prepared to order and well presented, with nothing but the freshest ingredients used throughout. Food is available at lunchtime and in the evening, until 10pm, Monday to Saturday and until 6.30pm on Sunday.

- 🕐 Mon-Sat 11.00-23.00; Sun 12.00-22.30
- 🍴 Homemade pub food with no frills
- 💷 Visa, Mastercard, Delta, Switch
- 🅿 Large beer garden, heated patio area, car park
- 🎵 Quiz on Tuesdays, pool table
- @ butchdog@tinyonline.co.uk
- ❓ Polesden Lacey 4 miles, Box Hill 4 miles, Epsom Downs Racecourse 3 miles, Chessington Zoo 4 miles, Hatchlands 7 miles, Guildford 12 miles

THE SHEPHERD AND FLOCK

22 MOOR PARK LANE, FARNHAM, SURREY GU9 9JB
TEL: 01252 716675 FAX: 01252 716053

> **Directions:** From junction 10 on the M25 take the A3 to Guildford and then the A31 to Farnham. The Shepherd and Flock lies on the outskirts of Farnham at the junction with the A287 on the Shepherd and Flock roundabout

Situated on a busy roundabout, **The Shepherd and Flock**, with its large lawned area to the front, is hard to miss whilst travelling round Farnham on the bypass. The pub has been here around 90 years, although it was originally housed in the cottage next door, and the roundabout on which it stands is said to be the most populated in Europe - there are 17 houses built on it as well as the inn!

Owners Stephen and Helen Hill came here in 1990 and in that time they have gradually transformed The Shepherd and

Flock into the high quality establishment that can be seen here today. The long central bar, with its open fire, has a real country feel and the adjacent dining area provides a pleasant atmosphere in which to enjoy the inn's excellent food, which is described as 'an experience'. Even the sandwiches here are a feast - made with fresh, thick crusty bread and oozing with juicy filling - and there is also a whole range of home-cooked traditional pub fayre from which to choose, with the innovative chef always striving to create new dishes with which to tempt the most jaded of palates. Stephen and Helen have certainly made a great success of their pub food but it is perhaps for the superb range of eight real ales that the inn is best known with regular mentions in the Good Beer Guide.

- 🕐 Mon-Thu 11.00-15.00, 17.30-23.00; Fri-Sat 11.00-23.00; Sun 12.00-22.30
- 🍴 Bar meals and snacks, traditional Sunday lunch
- £ Visa, Mastercard, Delta, Switch, Amex
- 🅿 Beer garden, car parking
- 🎵 Quiz on Tuesday nights, darts
- ❓ Farnham Castle, Waverley Abbey 2 miles, Bird World 3 miles, Jenkyn Place Gardens 4 miles, Farnborough 5 miles, Loseley House 8 miles, Guildford 10 miles

THE STAG ON THE RIVER

LOWER EASHING ROAD, EASHING, GODALMING, SURREY GU7 2QG
TEL: 01483 421568 FAX: 01483 861112

Directions: From junction 10 on the M25 take the A3 around Guildford and continue in the direction of Milford. Two miles after passing through Compton take the minor road to the left to the village of Eashing.

In an attractive riverside setting **The Stag on the River** is a wonderful old inn that dates back to the17th century, located in the heart of the tranquil village of Eashing within easy reach of the A3. Originally it was the Mill House but it has been much extended over the centuries resulting in an attractive structure that is well preserved and has become a listed building.

The Stag is, indeed, a delightful place to visit as not only is there a delightful garden and patio area overlooking the River Wey but the interior is comfortable, stylish and tasteful. The original brick and tile floors have been retained, together with large open fireplaces, and the many original features blend seamlessly with more modern touches creating a pleasing environment. Excellent food and drink are very much the order of the day here with a traditional menu of bar meals and snacks available for lunch, seven days a week. In the evening a full a la carte menu is also served with a superb selection of freshly prepared delicious sounding dishes. Seafood is a popular choice and to round off your meal to perfection, there is an exquisite collection of desserts. To make any evening extra special, then why not arrange to stay over in one of the two, comfortable en-suite guest rooms. Naturally, the accommodation is of the same exceptional standard.

- Mon-Sat 11.00-15.00, 18.00-23.00; Sun 12.00-15.00, 19.00-22.30
- Excellent menu ranging from bar snacks to full a la carte
- Visa, Mastercard, Delta, Switch
- 2 en-suite rooms
- Riverside garden, car park
- Witley Common 2 miles, Winkworth Arboretum 3 miles, Loseley House 3 miles, Godalming 1 mile, Guildford 4 miles, Polesden Lacey 14 miles

Surrey

THE STAR

MAIN ROAD, BENTLEY, NEAR FARNHAM, SURREY GU10 5LW
TEL/FAX: 01420 23184

Directions: From junction 5 on the M3 take the A287 to Farnham and then the A31 towards Alton. Approximately 4 miles from Farnham take the road signposted for Bentley to the right

If you happened to see any of the BB2 documentary, The Village, you will find Bentley, and **The Star** rather familiar. Though gaining some notoriety, life in the village and at this late-19th century pub remains much as it did before the cameras arrived and it is still a well frequented local that has served the needs of the villagers for many years. Old pictures of the village adorn the walls of the warm and inviting

🕐 Mon-Wed 12.00-15.00, 18.00-23.00; Thu-Sun 12.00-23.00

🍴 Bar meals and snacks, traditional Sunday lunches, Summer barbecues

£ Visa, Access, Delta, Switch

Ⓟ Large beer garden, children's play area, car park

🎵 Occasional live music

@ paul@starinnbentley.fsnet.co.uk

❓ Jenkyn Place Gardens, Farnham Castle 4 miles, Waverley Abbey 5 miles, Goose Green Trail 3 miles, Farnborough Airfield 9 miles, Jane Austen's House 7 miles

bar area where a wide range of drinks, including real ales, are served. You will also find a games room and a separate restaurant, all furnished for comfort and providing a homely, relaxed ambiance.

A well known and popular place for a drink and good conversation, The Star is also renowned for its excellent pub food that is available both at lunchtimes and most evenings (no food Sunday or Monday nights). The superb menu offers an excellent range of dishes from which to choose, all presented on blackboard menus, and regularly updated to make the most of seasonal produce. The games room offers a pool table and darts board for whiling away a wet afternoon, and there is also occasional live music.

THE STAR

17 CHURCH STREET, GODALMING, SURREY GU7 1EL
TEL: 01483 417717

> **Directions:** Leaving the M25 at junction 10, take the A3 south west to Guildford. In the centre of Guildford pick up the A3100 which will lead you directly to Godalming.

Since the 1800s, **The Star** has enjoyed a quiet location on a side street in Godalming, and it is a traditional, town centre inn with real charm that appeals to a wide ranging clientele. The atmosphere is relaxed and friendly and you can be sure of a warm welcome from the owners, Ian and Amanda Thomson, and their staff. Popular with locals both at lunchtime and in the evenings, you only have to venture inside to appreciate its full appeal, with the décor having an Irish theme giving it a cosy, slightly cluttered feel.

A menu of bar snacks and hot meals is served each lunchtime and evening, seven days a week, serving mainly classic dishes like your mother used to make.

Using the freshest of ingredients all meals are prepared to order and offer good value for money. To while away a sunny summer afternoon, or wet winter's evening, the pub can offer a boules terrain, bar billiards and other traditional pub games and there is usually live music to be enjoyed each Thursday night. In warm weather you can also make the most of the large garden located to the rear of the pub, where there are tables and chairs at which to sit.

- 🕐 Mon-Thurs 11.00-15.00, 17.00-23.00; Fri-Sat 11.00-23.00; Sun 12.00-22.30
- 🍴 Home-made, old fashioned dishes
- 💷 Visa, Mastercard, Delta, Switch
- Ⓟ Beer garden
- 🎵 Live music each Thursday
- ❓ Loseley House 2 miles, Winkworth Arboretum 3 miles, Guildford 4 miles, Albury Park 7 miles, Hatchlands House 10 miles, Farnham Castle 9 miles

THE STEPPING STONES

Surrey

WESTHUMBLE STREET, WESTHUMBLE, DORKING, SURREY RH5 6BS
TEL/FAX: 01306 889932

> **Directions:** Leave the M25 at junction 9 and take the A24 around Leatherhead towards Dorking. About a mile before you reach Dorking, the village of Westhumble will be signposted to the right

The Stepping Stones is a fine, large pub situated on a leafy lane, just off the A24, and conveniently located for those heading towards Gatwick Airport or the South coast. This is an affluent area, and the elegant building manages to

hold its own in a village which is full of prime residential property. The pub has been under the guidance of husband and wife team, Roger and Sharon Norminton for the past three years and their passion for the place shows through in all areas.

- Mon-Sat 11.00-15.00 and 17.00-23.00; Sun 12.00-22.30
- Bar meals and snacks at lunchtime with an a la carte evening menu
- Visa, Mastercard, Delta, Switch
- Car park, patio garden, children's play area
- Polesden Lacey 2 miles, Box Hill 1 mile, Ranmore Forest Walk 3 miles, Epsom Downs Racecourse 7 miles, Leith Hill Tower 6 miles, Guildford 12 miles

The interior has been kept open plan, enhancing the spacious feel, and furnished in a clean modern style reflecting the best of rural and city life. Popular with those living in the surrounding area, the superb restaurant attracts regular customers from far and wide. A superb menu of bar meals and snacks is served each lunchtime while in the evening the chefs show their true colours with a superb a la carte menu available Monday to Saturday nights. The cuisine is mainly traditional English, with influences from world cuisine showing through. The daily specials board offers some extra seasonal dishes with fresh fish often featuring.

THE SURREY OAKS

PARKGATE ROAD, NEWDIGATE, SURREY RH5 5DZ
TEL: 01306 631200 FAX: 01306 631200

> **Directions:** Leave the M25 at junction 8 and take the A217 to Reigate. Pick up the A25 heading west towards Dorking and after four miles turn left onto a minor road. Follow this for around 5 miles where you will find the Surrey Oak at Parkgate.

The original parts of **The Surrey Oaks** date from 1570 and although the pub has been extended over the centuries much of the historic character has been retained both inside and out. The setting, in the little village of Parkgate, tucked into a quiet corner of Surrey yet within easy reach of Guildford and Gatwick airport, is delightful and the attractive pub is surrounded by spectacular gardens. Inside, the Georgian bar has been converted into a restaurant, and there are two small, beamed bars,

one with an inglenook fireplace and stone-flagged floor.

The Surrey Oaks is a renowned real ale pub and a regular CAMRA award-winner though the food is an equally popular feature. Restaurant and bar menus offer a good range of dishes, plus daily specials from the blackboard, with the offerings including steaks, seafood, fresh fish, game, pasta and vegetarian options. Food is available in the bar area and the non-smoking restaurant between midday and 2pm seven days a week. Evening meals are served between 7pm and 9.30pm Tuesday to Saturday. The bar stocks four excellent real ales with two guest beers, a range of quality wines and specialist bottled beers from Belgium and Holland. A highlight of the calendar is the annual beer festival, held in August at the Bank Holiday weekend.

- 🕐 Mon-Fri 11.30-14.30, 17.30-23.00; Sat 11.30-15.00, 18.00-23.00; Sun 12.00-15.00, 19.00-22.30
- 🍴 Comprehensive restaurant and bar snack menu
- £ Visa, Access, Delta, Switch, Amex, Diners
- Ⓟ Large car park, beer garden, children's play area
- ♫ Occasional live music, annual beer festival
- @ e-mail: maccolyte@talk21.com website: www.surreyoaks.co.uk
- ? Gatwick Airport 6 miles, Box Hill 6 miles, Leith Hill Tower 7 miles, Polesden Lacey 9 miles, Nymans Gardens 12 miles, Guildford 16 miles

THE SWAN

PETWORTH ROAD, CHIDDINGFOLD, SURREY GU8 4TY
TEL: 01428 682073

Directions: Leave the M25 at junction 10 and follow the A3 towards Guildford and beyond. At Milford bear left onto the A283 and you will reach the village of Chiddingfold after around 4 miles.

Situated in the village of Chiddingfold on the Petworth Road, **The Swan Inn** has been completely refurbished by the proprietor Daniel Hall in the 18 months since he arrived here. Dating back to the 15th century, this former coaching inn has been restored to its former glory and it continues to cater to both the locals and weary travellers, serving superb home cooked food, real ales, and a wide selection of wines to suit all tastes. There is plenty of car parking available opposite the inn, to the rear visitors will find extensive terraced gardens, while inside a warm, friendly welcome awaits. The light and airy public bar is attractively furnished with leather settees and chunky rustic furniture and the exquisite restaurant is a haven of white linen tablecloths, polished silver cutlery and sparkling crystal. Here you can sample some delicious dishes from a superb menu prepared by classically trained chefs that are passionate about fresh fish, shellfish and local game. There is a wide ranging wine list and Daniel is always happy to advise in selecting the best according to your menu and personal taste.

You will find bed and breakfast accommodation available here, making The Swan Inn the ideal venue to spend a relaxing and memorable week-end or stop-over.

- Mon-Fri 11.00-15.00; 17.30-23.00; Sat 11.00-23.00; Sun 12.00-22.30
- Superb restaurant served top quality food
- Visa, Mastercard, Delta, Switch, Amex
- 3 en-suite rooms, with more planned
- Nearby car parking
- e-mail: theswan@chiddingfold.fsnet.co.uk website: www.swaninnandrestaurant.co.uk
- Black Down Nature Trail 4 miles, Winkworth Arboretum 7 miles, Hascombe Court Gardens 6 miles, Thursley Nature Reserve 6 miles, Guildford 8 miles

THE WHARF

WHARF STREET, GODALMING, SURREY GU7 1NN
TEL: 01483 419543 FAX: 01483 419951

Directions: Leaving the M25 at junction 10, take the A3 south west to Guildford. In the centre of Guildford pick up the A3100 which will lead you directly to Godalming.

The Wharf enjoys a superb town centre location, positioned just a few yards from the main shopping street. Dating back to the 1800s, the terraced property was once the British Legion Club. The whole place has been revamped by the current owner Tim Hughes who has only been here a year, and already created a more contemporary environment that has proved to be highly popular. The long, narrow bar features oak floors, tall tables and cosy alcoves, all uncluttered and spacious, while retaining some of the more interesting features of the original building.

Of course, it isn't just the ambiance that people come here for – the bar also offers a popular range of liquid refreshment with real ales, premium beers, an extensive wine list and top quality Costa coffee served all day too. The food is pretty good too, with a wide selection of fresh, simple hot and cold dishes, ranging from pasta and burgers, to fish and spicy chilli. There are also lots of snacks and sandwiches to choose from as well, with hot panini and coffee available for take away. Additional facilities include an internet kiosk, and for the big kids among you, some giant games including Jenga and Connect Four.

- 🕐 Mon-Sat 12.00-23.00; Sun 19.00-22.30
- 🍴 Simple, light meals served all day
- 💷 Visa, Mastercard, Delta, Switch
- 🅿 Internet kiosk
- 🎵 Pub games
- @ wharfgodalming@bt.com
- ❓ Winkworth Arboretum 3 miles, Hascombe Court Gardens 3 miles, Guildford 4 miles, Sutton Place 8 miles, Waverley Abbey 8 miles, Farnham Castle 9 miles

THE WHEATSHEAF

HIGH STREET, BRAMLEY, SURREY GU5 0HB
TEL: 01483 892722

> **Directions:** Leaving the M25 at junction 10, follow the A3 into Guildford then pick up the A281 road heading towards Horsham. A few miles beyond Guildford you will find yourself in Bramley.

The Wheatsheaf is a traditional 16th-century village inn which is well placed within the busy village of Bramley. It retains the original old windows and doors, which together with the colourful window boxes present an attractive, welcoming appearance. Inside the décor is pleasant and cosy, with a carpeted lounge bar area and oak beams adding to the characterful feel and the main bar being bright and warm and kept spotlessly clean. The high standards are maintained by current owners, William and Jeayne, with William having previously been a builder, taking on the pub for a more relaxing life! Due to the couple's hard work in all areas,

The Wheatsheaf has regained its popularity with the locals and also attracts a number of people who are simply passing through.

Home cooked food is served lunchtimes and Sunday to Thursday evenings with a roast available at Sunday lunch. The menu offers the usual choices of bar snacks and hot dishes, all simply presented, in hearty portions and offering great value for money. A games room with pool table and fortnightly live performers provide the opportunity for a more lively evening out, and if you want to stop overnight there are three guest rooms available for bed and breakfast. At the time of writing there are plans for a further two rooms, so simply ring for full details and availability.

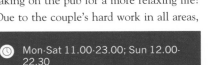

- 🕐 Mon-Sat 11.00-23.00; Sun 12.00-22.30
- 🍴 Tasty bar food
- 💷 Visa, Mastercard, Delta, Switch
- 🛏 3 rooms with en-suite showers
- 🅿 Beer garden
- 🎵 Live music fortnightly, pool table
- ❓ Guildford 4 miles, Winkworth Arboretum 3 miles, Albury Park 5 miles, Leith Hill Tower 11 miles, Loseley House 3 miles, Hatchlands 8 miles, Polesden Lacey 12 miles

WILLIAM IV

LITTLE COMMON LANE, BLETCHINGLEY, REDHILL, SURREY RH1 4QF
TEL: 01883 743278

> **Directions:** Leave the M25 at junction 6 heading into Godstone. The village of Bletchingley can be found just two miles to the west, following the A25 Redhill road.

The **William IV** is a charming, unspoilt Victorian pub hidden away on a quiet lane just off the A25 and within easy reach of the motorway. Built on a slope, the front door is reached by a set of steps, and the neat, tidy exterior gives no clues as to what you are going to find within. Should you venture inside you will discover a tiny public bar, an adjoining lounge bar together with a non-smoking restaurant. Cosy to the extreme, it is the landlady Su Saunders and her sons who have brought the essential touch to ensure a welcome feel to the place.

In the restaurant you can enjoy fine home cooking with the varied menus available each lunchtime, evening and all day on Sunday until 9pm. The traditional, mainly English, cuisine

ranges from pies, steaks and lasagne to fresh fish and delicious pizzas. The prices are reasonable too, and sure to please every pocket. Children are made more than welcome in the eating areas until early evening, and you will find on the menu some dishes specially designed for younger tastes and appetites. The bar is well stocked and offers an excellent range of real ales including Harveys Best and the locally brewed Pilgrim's Progress. Outside you will find a sizeable beer garden and plenty of car parking.

- 🕐 Mon-Sat 12.00-15.00, 18.00-23.00; Sun 12.00-22.30
- 🍴 Excellent, wholesome, home-cooked food
- £ Visa, Access, Delta, Switch
- 🅿 Beer garden, car park
- 🎵 Monthly quiz nights
- ❓ Nutfield Priory 2 miles, Detillers House 5 miles, Quebec House 9 miles, Polesden Lacey 13 miles, Gatwick Airport 9 miles, Box Hill 12 miles

Surrey

THE WOBURN ARMS

ADDLESTONE MOOR, ADDLESTONE, NR. WEYBRIDGE,
SURREY KT15 2QH
TEL: 01932 563314

> **Directions:** Leave the M25 at junction 11 and head towards Weybridge. At first
> roundabout take second exit for Addlestone Moor.

The Woburn Arms is a large, sprawling establishment dating from just after the war, although there have been records of a pub on the site since 1865. Conveniently situated just a stone's throw from the motorway, there is a sizeable car park,

making this an ideal place to take a break from the stresses and strains of the M25. The interior is spacious and has a

- Mon-Sat 11.00-23.00; Sun 12.00-22.30
- Bar food and restaurant
- Visa, Mastercard, Delta, Switch
- Beer garden, car park
- Disco Thursday-Sunday nights, Quiz Tuesdays, pool table
- @ steve.milnes@virgin.net
- ? Sandown Park Racecourse 7 miles, R.H.S. Wisley Gardens 4 miles, Guildford 11 miles, Windsor Castle 10 miles, Hampton Court Palace 10 miles

well worn and comfortable feel, and the young couple Steve and Fran Milnes, will undoubtedly make you feel very welcome. The regular clientele is a mixture of all ages - there are discos every weekend playing a variety of popular music, but for a more sedate evening out you could pit your wits against the locals in a friendly pub quiz, held each Tuesday.

The bar is suitably stocked with beers and lagers, with real ale also kept on tap. Tasty home-cooked style food is available with separate lunch and evening menus Monday to Saturday (a la carte Saturday Night) and traditional roast on Sunday lunch.

THE WOOLPACK

THE GREEN, ELSTEAD, NR. GODALMING, SURREY GU8 6HD
TEL: 01252 703106 FAX: 01252 703497

Directions: Leaving the M25 at junction 10, take the A3 south west. About 5 miles beyond Guildford turn right onto the B3001 and you will reach the village of Elstead after around 2 miles.

The Woolpack can be found located by the village green in the heart of Elstead, midway between the old sheep market towns of Godalming and Farnham. It started life as a barn and became an inn in the 16ᵗʰ century when it was used by herders as a place to rest and refresh themselves on the way to market, leaving their sheep to graze on the common land. Visitors today will find a low beamed interior with open log fires, furnished with settles, spindle back chairs and plain tables. The traditional décor is enhanced by the use of paraphernalia from the wool industry, such as spindles and bobbins.

The bar is dominated by racks of cask ale, with dried hops overhead, and the fine, well-kept ales are served direct from the casks. There is also an excellent range of food, with the menu presented on blackboards, offering a continually changing selection of old English and colonial dishes. Everything is served in generous portions and there is a wonderful display of tempting home-made puddings to round off your meal.

This part of Surrey is a rambler's heaven with 500 acres of common and heathland to explore in an area of outstanding natural beauty, with over 80 kms of footpaths and bridleways. There are also many designated sites of special scientific interest. If you are exploring the area with 'man's best friend', dogs on leads are welcome in the bar and garden room.

Kevin and Sally Macready and their team (some here for 16 years!) promote a warm, friendly, informal and welcoming atmosphere. So you can eat, drink, relax, and be merry.

🕐 Mon-Fri 11.00-15.00, 17.30-23.00; Sat 11.00-23.00; Sun 12.00-22.30

🍴 Inventive menus serving olde English cuisine

£ Visa, Mastercard, Delta, Switch

Ⓟ Beer garden, car park

@ kevin.macready@whsmithnet.co.uk

? Thursley Nature Reserve 2 miles, Loseley House 6 miles, Winkworth Arboretum 7 miles, Guildford 7 miles, Farnham Castle 5 miles, Waverley Abbey 4 miles

ALPHABETICAL LIST
OF PUBS AND INNS

E

F

G

H

K

L

M

O

T

W

Y

Alphabetical List of Pubs and Inns

SPECIAL INTEREST LISTS

Accommodation

KENT

SUSSEX

SURREY

SPECIAL INTEREST LISTS

SPECIAL INTEREST LISTS

All Day Opening

KENT

The Albion Tavern	Faversham, Kent	25
Black Horse	Pluckley, Kent	30
The Black Horse	Canterbury, Kent	31
The Castle Inn	Chiddingstone, Kent	33
The Cinque Ports Arms	New Romney, Kent	34
Eight Bells	Hawkhurst, Kent	37
The Four Elms Inn	Four Elms, Edenbridge, Kent	39
George Hotel	Lydd, Kent	41
Half Moon	Hildenborough, Tonbridge, Kent	44
Hare and Hounds	Blean, Canterbury, Kent	45
Hodden on the Hill	Ashford, Kent	46
The Hop Pickers	Hothfield, Ashford, Kent	47
The King Henry VIII	Hever, Edenbridge, Kent	48
Kings Arms	Boxley, Kent	49
The Lord Nelson	Dover, Kent	51
Man of Kent	Tonbridge, Kent	52
Olde Kings Head	Hothfield, Ashford, Kent	53
Pied Bull	Farningham, Kent	54
The Pilot	Maidstone, Kent	55
The Pinnacles	Tonbridge, Kent	56
The Queens Head	Mereworth, Kent	59
The Queens Head	Sutton Valence, Kent	60
The Sportsman	Cliffsend, Ramsgate, Kent	63
The Star Inn	Westwood, Broadstairs, Kent	65
The Swan	Great Chart, Ashford, Kent	67
The Swan	Teynham, Sittingbourne, Kent	68
The Two Sawyers	Woolage Green, Canterbury, Kent	70
Walnut Tree	East Farleigh, Kent	71
Westbere Butts	Sturry, Canterbury, Kent	73
The Wheatsheaf	Kemsing, Sevenoaks, Kent	74
Wheatsheaf Inn	Marsh Green, Edenbridge, Kent	75
The White Horse Inn	Sundridge, Sevenoaks, Kent	77
White Horse Inn	Hawkinge, Folkestone, Kent	78

All Day Opening

SUSSEX

The Beach Tavern	Pevensey Bay, East Sussex	104
The Bell Inn	Iden, Rye, East Sussex	105
Charcoal Burner	Furnice Green, Crawley, West Sussex	108
Malt Shovel	Horsham, West Sussex	111
The Olde Bell Inn	Rye, East Sussex	112
The Park Tavern	Chichester, West Sussex	113
Prince of Wales	Heathfield, East Sussex	115
The Ram Inn	Firle, Lewes, East Sussex	116
Rose and Crown	Burwash, East Sussex	117
The Royal Oak	Pett, Hastings, East Sussex	120
The Sussex Oak	Warnham, Horsham, West Sussex	122
Windsor Tavern	Eastbourne, East Sussex	123
Ye Olde House at Home	Broadwater, Worthing, West Sussex	124

SURREY

The Abinger Arms	Abinger Hammer, Surrey	146
The Admiral	Reigate, Surrey	147
The Canbury Arms	Kingston upon Thames, Surrey	150
The Compasses Inn	Gomshall, Guildford, Surrey	151
Crouch Oak	Addlestone, Surrey	153
Duke's Head	Tadworth, Surrey	154
The Parrot Inn	Dorking, Surrey	157
The Pilgrim	Dorking, Surrey	158
The Plough	Coldharbour, Dorking, Surrey	159
The Red Cross Inn	Reigate, Surrey	161
Red Lion	Godalming, Surrey	162
Red Lion	Thames Ditton, Surrey	163
The Royal Oak	Stonebridge, Dorking, Surrey	164
The Running Horse	Leatherhead, Surrey	165
The Wharf	Godalming, Surrey	173
The Wheatsheaf	Bramley, Surrey	174
The Woburn Arms	Addlestone, Surrey	176

Childrens Facilities

KENT

SUSSEX

SURREY

SPECIAL INTEREST LISTS

Credit Cards Accepted

KENT

The Albion Tavern	Faversham, Kent	25
The Alma	Painters Forstal, Faversham, Kent	26
Anchor & Hope	New Ash Green, Kent	27
The Bell Inn	Minster-In-Thanet, Kent	29
Black Horse	Pluckley, Kent	30
The Castle Inn	Chiddingstone, Kent	33
The Cinque Ports Arms	New Romney, Kent	34
The Cock Horse	Hildenborough, Tonbridge, Kent	35
The Dirty Habit	Hollingbourne, Maidstone, Kent	36
Eight Bells	Hawkhurst, Kent	37
Fleur-de-Lis	Leigh, Tonbridge, Kent	38
The Four Elms Inn	Four Elms, Edenbridge, Kent	39
George Hotel	Lydd, Kent	41
George Inn	Molash, Canterbury, Kent	42
Green Cross Inn	Goudhurst, Kent	43
Half Moon	Hildenborough, Tonbridge, Kent	44
Hare and Hounds	Blean, Canterbury, Kent	45
Hodden on the Hill	Ashford, Kent	46
The Hop Pickers	Hothfield, Ashford, Kent	47
The King Henry VIII	Hever, Edenbridge, Kent	48
Kings Arms	Boxley, Kent	49
Kings Arms	Elham, Canterbury, Kent	50
Man of Kent	Tonbridge, Kent	52
Pied Bull	Farningham, Kent	54
The Pinnacles	Tonbridge, Kent	56
The Plough	Trottiscliffe, West Malling, Kent	57
The Plough & Great Barn	Hildenborough, Tonbridge, Kent	58
The Queens Head	Sutton Valence, Kent	60
The Red Cow	Sandwich, Kent	61
The Red Lion	Rustall, Royal Tunbridge Wells, Kent	62
The Stanhope Arms	Brasted, Kent	64
Sugar Loaves	Hollingbourne, Kent	66
The Swan	Great Chart, Ashford, Kent	67
Tudor Rose	Borden, Sittingbourne, Kent	69
Walnut Tree	East Farleigh, Kent	71
The Walnut Tree	Aldington, Ashford, Kent	72
Westbere Butts	Sturry, Canterbury, Kent	73

Credit Cards Accepted

The Wheatsheaf	Kemsing, Sevenoaks, Kent	74
Wheatsheaf Inn	Marsh Green, Edenbridge, Kent	75
The White Horse Inn	Sundridge, Sevenoaks, Kent	77
White Horse Inn	Hawkinge, Folkestone, Kent	78
The Windmill	Hollingbourne, Kent	79

SUSSEX

The Alma	Uckfield, East Sussex	102
Bax Castle	Southwater, Horsham, West Sussex	103
The Bell Inn	Iden, Rye, East Sussex	105
The Brewers Arms	Herstmonceux, East Sussex	106
Charcoal Burner	Furnice Green, Crawley, West Sussex	108
Foresters Arms	Kirdford, Billingshurst, West Sussex	109
The Lamb Inn	Wartling, Hailsham, East Sussex	110
Malt Shovel	Horsham, West Sussex	111
The Park Tavern	Chichester, West Sussex	113
The Plough	Crawley, West Sussex	114
Prince of Wales	Heathfield, East Sussex	115
The Ram Inn	Firle, Lewes, East Sussex	116
Rose and Crown	Burwash, East Sussex	117
Rose and Crown	Pulborough, West Sussex	118
Royal Oak	Barcombe, Lewes, East Sussex	119
The Royal Oak	Pett, Hastings, East Sussex	120
The Smuggler	Pett, Hastings, East Sussex	121
The Sussex Oak	Warnham, Horsham, West Sussex	122
Ye Olde House at Home	Broadwater, Worthing, West Sussex	124
Ye White Harte Inne	Cuckfield, West Sussex	125

SURREY

The Abinger Arms	Abinger Hammer, Surrey	146
The Blacksmiths Head	Newchapel, Lingfield, Surrey	148
The British Volunteer	Weybridge, Surrey	149
The Canbury Arms	Kingston upon Thames, Surrey	150
The Compasses Inn	Gomshall, Guildford, Surrey	151
The Cricketers	Cobham, Surrey	152
Crouch Oak	Addlestone, Surrey	153
Duke's Head	Tadworth, Surrey	154
Half Moon	Windlesham, Surrey	155
The Parrot Inn	Dorking, Surrey	157
The Pilgrim	Dorking, Surrey	158

Credit Cards Accepted

SURREY (Cont.)

The Plough	Coldharbour, Dorking, Surrey	159
The Ram's Nest Inn	Chiddingfold, Surrey	160
The Red Cross Inn	Reigate, Surrey	161
Red Lion	Godalming, Surrey	162
Red Lion	Thames Ditton, Surrey	163
The Royal Oak	Stonebridge, Dorking, Surrey	164
The Running Horse	Leatherhead, Surrey	165
The Shepherd and Flock	Farnham, Surrey	166
The Stag on the River	Eashing, Godalming, Surrey	167
The Star	Bentley, Farnham, Surrey	168
The Star	Godalming, Surrey	169
The Stepping Stones	Westhumble, Dorking, Surrey	170
The Surrey Oaks	Newdigate, Surrey	171
The Swan	Chiddingfold, Surrey	172
The Wharf	Godalming, Surrey	173
The Wheatsheaf	Bramley, Surrey	174
William IV	Bletchingley, Redhill, Surrey	175
The Woburn Arms	Addlestone, Surrey	176
The Woolpack	Elstead, Godalming, Surrey	177

Garden, Patio or Terrace

KENT

The Albion Tavern	Faversham, Kent	25
The Alma	Painters Forstal, Faversham, Kent	26
Anchor & Hope	New Ash Green, Kent	27
The Artichoke	Chartham, Canterbury, Kent	28
The Bell Inn	Minster-In-Thanet, Kent	29
Black Horse	Pluckley, Kent	30
The Black Horse	Canterbury, Kent	31
Castle Inn	Oare, Faversham, Kent	32
The Castle Inn	Chiddingstone, Kent	33
The Cinque Ports Arms	New Romney, Kent	34
The Cock Horse	Hildenborough, Tonbridge, Kent	35
The Dirty Habit	Hollingbourne, Maidstone, Kent	36
Eight Bells	Hawkhurst, Kent	37
Fleur-de-Lis	Leigh, Tonbridge, Kent	38
The Four Elms Inn	Four Elms, Edenbridge, Kent	39
Fox and Hounds	Toys Hill, Edenbridge, Kent	40
George Hotel	Lydd, Kent	41
George Inn	Molash, Canterbury, Kent	42
Green Cross Inn	Goudhurst, Kent	43
Half Moon	Hildenborough, Tonbridge, Kent	44
Hare and Hounds	Blean, Canterbury, Kent	45
Hodden on the Hill	Ashford, Kent	46
The Hop Pickers	Hothfield, Ashford, Kent	47
The King Henry VIII	Hever, Edenbridge, Kent	48
Kings Arms	Boxley, Kent	49
Kings Arms	Elham, Canterbury, Kent	50
The Lord Nelson	Dover, Kent	51
Man of Kent	Tonbridge, Kent	52
Olde Kings Head	Hothfield, Ashford, Kent	53
Pied Bull	Farningham, Kent	54
The Pilot	Maidstone, Kent	55
The Pinnacles	Tonbridge, Kent	56
The Plough	Trottiscliffe, West Malling, Kent	57
The Plough & Great Barn	Hildenborough, Tonbridge, Kent	58
The Queens Head	Mereworth, Kent	59
The Queens Head	Sutton Valence, Kent	60
The Red Cow	Sandwich, Kent	61

Garden, Patio or Terrace

KENT (Cont.)

The Red Lion	Rustall, Royal Tunbridge Wells, Kent	62
The Sportsman	Cliffsend, Ramsgate, Kent	63
The Stanhope Arms	Brasted, Kent	64
The Star Inn	Westwood, Broadstairs, Kent	65
Sugar Loaves	Hollingbourne, Kent	66
The Swan	Great Chart, Ashford, Kent	67
The Swan	Teynham, Sittingbourne, Kent	68
Tudor Rose	Borden, Sittingbourne, Kent	69
The Two Sawyers	Woolage Green, Canterbury, Kent	70
Walnut Tree	East Farleigh, Kent	71
The Walnut Tree	Aldington, Ashford, Kent	72
Westbere Butts	Sturry, Canterbury, Kent	73
The Wheatsheaf	Kemsing, Sevenoaks, Kent	74
Wheatsheaf Inn	Marsh Green, Edenbridge, Kent	75
The White Horse Inn	Sundridge, Sevenoaks, Kent	77
White Horse Inn	Hawkinge, Folkestone, Kent	78
The Windmill	Hollingbourne, Kent	79

SUSSEX

The Alma	Uckfield, East Sussex	102
Bax Castle	Southwater, Horsham, West Sussex	103
The Beach Tavern	Pevensey Bay, East Sussex	104
The Bell Inn	Iden, Rye, East Sussex	105
The Brewers Arms	Herstmonceux, East Sussex	106
Catts Inn	Rotherfield, East Sussex	107
Charcoal Burner	Furnice Green, Crawley, West Sussex	108
Foresters Arms	Kirdford, Billingshurst, West Sussex	109
The Lamb Inn	Wartling, Hailsham, East Sussex	110
Malt Shovel	Horsham, West Sussex	111
The Olde Bell Inn	Rye, East Sussex	112
The Plough	Crawley, West Sussex	114
Prince of Wales	Heathfield, East Sussex	115
The Ram Inn	Firle, Lewes, East Sussex	116
Rose and Crown	Burwash, East Sussex	117
Rose and Crown	Pulborough, West Sussex	118
Royal Oak	Barcombe, Lewes, East Sussex	119
The Royal Oak	Pett, Hastings, East Sussex	120
The Smuggler	Pett, Hastings, East Sussex	121
The Sussex Oak	Warnham, Horsham, West Sussex	122

SUSSEX (Cont.)

SURREY

SPECIAL INTEREST LISTS

Live Entertainment

KENT

SUSSEX

Live Entertainment

SURREY

SPECIAL INTEREST LISTS

Restaurant or Dining Area

KENT

The Alma	Painters Forstal, Faversham, Kent	26
The Artichoke	Chartham, Canterbury, Kent	28
Black Horse	Pluckley, Kent	30
Castle Inn	Oare, Faversham, Kent	32
The Castle Inn	Chiddingstone, Kent	33
The Cinque Ports Arms	New Romney, Kent	34
The Cock Horse	Hildenborough, Tonbridge, Kent	35
Eight Bells	Hawkhurst, Kent	37
Fleur-de-Lis	Leigh, Tonbridge, Kent	38
The Four Elms Inn	Four Elms, Edenbridge, Kent	39
Fox and Hounds	Toys Hill, Edenbridge, Kent	40
George Hotel	Lydd, Kent	41
George Inn	Molash, Canterbury, Kent	42
Green Cross Inn	Goudhurst, Kent	43
Half Moon	Hildenborough, Tonbridge, Kent	44
Hare and Hounds	Blean, Canterbury, Kent	45
The Hop Pickers	Hothfield, Ashford, Kent	47
The King Henry VIII	Hever, Edenbridge, Kent	48
Kings Arms	Elham, Canterbury, Kent	50
Olde Kings Head	Hothfield, Ashford, Kent	53
The Pilot	Maidstone, Kent	55
The Pinnacles	Tonbridge, Kent	56
The Plough	Trottiscliffe, West Malling, Kent	57
The Red Cow	Sandwich, Kent	61
The Red Lion	Rustall, Royal Tunbridge Wells, Kent	62
The Stanhope Arms	Brasted, Kent	64
Tudor Rose	Borden, Sittingbourne, Kent	69
The Two Sawyers	Woolage Green, Canterbury, Kent	70
The Walnut Tree	Aldington, Ashford, Kent	72
Westbere Butts	Sturry, Canterbury, Kent	73
The Wheatsheaf	Kemsing, Sevenoaks, Kent	74
Wheatsheaf Inn	Marsh Green, Edenbridge, Kent	75

SUSSEX

Bax Castle	Southwater, Horsham, West Sussex	103
The Beach Tavern	Pevensey Bay, East Sussex	104
The Bell Inn	Iden, Rye, East Sussex	105

SUSSEX (CONT.)

SURREY

Places of Interest

PLACES OF INTEREST

Travel Publishing

The Hidden Places

Regional and National guides to the less well-known places of interest and places to eat, stay and drink

Hidden Inns

Regional guides to traditional pubs and inns throughout the United Kingdom

Regional and National guides to 18 hole golf courses and local places to stay, eat and drink

RURAL GUIDES

Regional and National guides to the traditional countryside of Britain and Ireland with easy to read facts on places to visit, stay, eat, drink and shop

For more information:

Phone: 0118 981 7777
Fax: 0118 982 0077
e-mail: adam@travelpublishing.co.uk **website:** www.travelpublishing.co.uk

Easy-to-use, Informative
Travel Guides on the British Isles

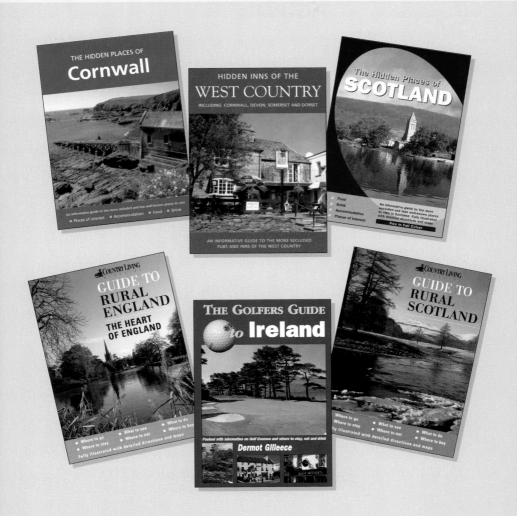

Travel Publishing Limited

7a Apollo House • Calleva Park • Aldermaston • Berkshire RG7 8TN

ORDER FORM

To order any of our publications just fill in the payment details below and complete the order form. For orders of less than 4 copies please add £1 per book for postage and packing. Orders over 4 copies are P & P free.

Please Complete Either:

I enclose a cheque for £ [ ] made payable to Travel Publishing Ltd

Or:

Card No: [ ] Expiry Date: [ ]

Signature: [ ]

Name: [ ]

Address: [ ]

Tel no: [ ]

Please either send, telephone, fax or e-mail your order to:

Travel Publishing Ltd, 7a Apollo House, Calleva Park, Aldermaston, Berkshire RG7 8TN   Tel: 0118 981 7777   Fax: 0118 982 0077
e-mail: karen@travelpublishing.co.uk

	Price	Quantity
Hidden Places Regional Titles		
Cambs & Lincolnshire	£7.99	....
Chilterns	£7.99	....
Cornwall	£8.99	....
Derbyshire	£8.99	....
Devon	£8.99	....
Dorset, Hants & Isle of Wight	£8.99	....
East Anglia	£8.99	....
Gloucs, Wiltshire & Somerset	£8.99	....
Heart of England	£7.99	....
Hereford, Worcs & Shropshire	£7.99	....
Highlands & Islands	£7.99	....
Kent	£8.99	....
Lake District & Cumbria	£8.99	....
Lancashire & Cheshire	£8.99	....
Lincolnshire & Notts	£8.99	....
Northumberland & Durham	£8.99	....
Sussex	£8.99	....
Yorkshire	£8.99	....
Hidden Places National Titles		
England	£10.99	....
Ireland	£10.99	....
Scotland	£10.99	....
Wales	£9.99	....

	Price	Quantity
Hidden Inns Titles		
East Anglia	£5.99	....
Heart of England	£5.99	....
Lancashire & Cheshire	£5.99	....
North of England	£5.99	....
South	£5.99	....
South East	£5.99	....
South and Central Scotland	£5.99	....
Wales	£5.99	....
Welsh Borders	£5.99	....
West Country	£5.99	....
Yorkshire	£5.99	....
Country Living Rural Guides		
East Anglia	£9.99	....
Heart of England	£9.99	....
Ireland	£10.99	....
Scotland	£10.99	....
South of England	£9.99	....
South East of England	£9.99	....
Wales	£10.99	....
West Country	£9.99	....

Total Quantity [ ]

Post & Packing [ ]

Total Value [ ]

READER REACTION FORM

The *Travel Publishing* research team would like to receive reader's comments on any visitor attractions or places reviewed in the book and also recommendations for suitable entries to be included in the next edition. This will help ensure that the *Country Living series of Rural Guides* continues to provide its readers with useful information on the more interesting, unusual or unique features of each attraction or place ensuring that their visit to the local area is an enjoyable and stimulating experience. To provide your comments or recommendations would you please complete the forms below and overleaf as indicated and send to:

**The Research Department, Travel Publishing Ltd,
7a Apollo House, Calleva Park, Aldermaston, Reading, RG7 8TN.**

Your Name:

Your Address:

Your Telephone Number:

Please tick as appropriate:

Comments ☐   Recommendation ☐

Name of Establishment:

Address:

Telephone Number:

Name of Contact:

READER REACTION FORM

Comment or Reason for Recommendation:

READER REACTION FORM

The *Travel Publishing* research team would like to receive reader's comments on any visitor attractions or places reviewed in the book and also recommendations for suitable entries to be included in the next edition. This will help ensure that the *Country Living series of Rural Guides* continues to provide its readers with useful information on the more interesting, unusual or unique features of each attraction or place ensuring that their visit to the local area is an enjoyable and stimulating experience. To provide your comments or recommendations would you please complete the forms below and overleaf as indicated and send to:

**The Research Department, Travel Publishing Ltd,
7a Apollo House, Calleva Park, Aldermaston, Reading, RG7 8TN.**

Your Name:

Your Address:

Your Telephone Number:

Please tick as appropriate:

Comments ☐   Recommendation ☐

Name of Establishment:

Address:

Telephone Number:

Name of Contact:

READER REACTION FORM

Comment or Reason for Recommendation: